One Smart Cookie

ONE SMART COOKIE

All your favorite cookies, squares, brownies and biscotti . . . *with less fat!*

Julie Van Rosendaal

whitecap

BOOK DESIGN BY Michelle Mayne
PHOTOGRAPHY & FOOD STYLING BY
Julie Van Rosendaal & Meg Van Rosendaal
EDITED BY Julie Van Rosendaal
& Meg Van Rosendaal
PROOFREAD BY Ben D'Andrea

Printed in Canada

Library and Archives Canada Cataloguing in Publication

Van Rosendaal, Julie, 1970-

One smart cookie : all your favorite cookies, squares, brownies and biscotti...with less fat! / Julie Van Rosendaal. -- Rev. & updated.

Includes index.

ISBN 978-1-55285-912-4
ISBN 1-55285-912-6

1. Cookies. 2. Low-fat diet--Recipes. I. Title.

TX772.R658 2007   641.8'654
C2007-901702-9

Nutritional analysis has been calculated using the Food Smart Business Edition program. When a choice is given, the analysis is based on the first listed ingredient. Optional ingredients are not included. When mixed dried fruit is called for, analysis is based on equal amounts of raisins, dried apricots and dried cranberries. When milk is called for, 1% milk is used in the analysis.

The publisher acknowledges the financial support of the Government of Canada through the Book Publishing Industry Development Program (BPIDP) and the province of British Columbia through the Book Publishing Tax Credit.

for Grandad

*who gave me
my entrepreneurial spirit*

for Grandma

*with whom I developed
my love for cooking*

ROLLED COOKIES | page 83

ICEBOX COOKIES | page 95

BISCOTTI | page 109

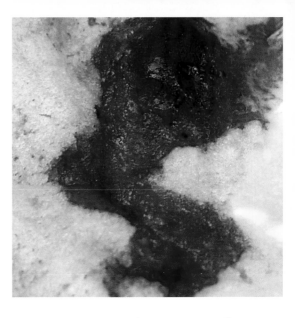

Introduction

This book represents years of kitchen testing by a food addict and cookie lover who was tired of the guilt trip that always followed a batch of homemade cookies.

I should say that my dad was my inspiration. Although cooking has always been my first love, I might never have ventured into the world of low-fat cooking if he didn't have the unfortunate combination of high cholesterol and a severe sweet tooth. Back when low-fat baking was in its infancy and the only desserts to be found in "healthy" cookbooks were meringues, poached fruit and the occasional oatmeal cookie made with applesauce, I decided to earn a few brownie points and develop some really good, rich, chewy, chocolatey cookies for him. After more testing than I care to admit, I came up with a winner, which my nephew dubbed Chocolava (see page 65) for its crinkly appearance. Even people who didn't care about fat and calories went wild for them, which was the whole point. I didn't think anyone should have to choose between a good cookie and a healthier one.

So I went into business and almost overnight was supplying over 50 restaurants, coffee shops and health clubs with low-fat chocolava, oatmeal-raisin and chocolate chip cookies.

Their popularity was overwhelming. I had requests for cookies from across Canada and even as far away as California. But the appeal of getting up at 1 o'clock in the morning to crank out cookies all night quickly wore off. I decided to close the bakery and write a cookbook, and at the same time develop recipes for all my favorite foods with less fat and fewer calories. After all, if it can be done with chocolate chip cookies, anything's possible!

At that point in my life I could no longer ignore the numbers on the scale. At 330+ pounds (my scale went up only to 330) I had tried every diet in the world with little progress. After all, the success rate of any diet program is a discouraging 5%, and I never liked to be told what I could and couldn't eat, and when. I hated the rigid calorie-calculating programs that expected me to weigh, measure and record everything that went into my mouth. Above all, I realized that guilt was a terrible motivator.

Once I learned to cook and eat on my own terms, making things like cookies, brownies and even butter tarts with less fat and fewer calories (like my dad, I was never willing to give up sweets or settle for unsatisfying low-fat versions) I finally succeeded in losing half my body weight — 165 pounds.

Cookies are the ultimate comfort food. What a shame that such pure enjoyment is often overshadowed by remorse over eating too much fat and too many calories! Fortunately there's no need to choose between a healthy cookie and a delicious one. By using healthier

ingredients and cooking techniques and moderating our intake, we can enjoy cookies regularly as part of a healthy lifestyle, rather than save them for an occasional treat.

The recipes in this book reflect the new attitude of cooks and food lovers who are concerned as much with taste as they are with nutrition. As we become more health-conscious and nutritionally savvy, we better understand what our bodies need to be healthy. But eating healthfully doesn't mean we should enjoy our food any less! Often considered "empty calories," cookies can deliver a bigger nutritional punch than we give them credit for.

I'm living proof that simple changes in eating habits and a common sense lifestyle can result in long-term success. I hope my book helps to change the way you bake and alleviates any guilt — and that these recipes become favorites in your home.

Julie Van Rosendaal

Baking Low-Fat Cookies: What's the Secret?

Cutting back on fat in your everyday cooking isn't difficult, but baking is another matter. Baking is more of a science, and fat plays an integral role, adding and enhancing flavor but also acting as a tenderizer in cookies, muffins, brownies and cakes. While many muffins, quick breads and cakes use healthier oils, most cookies rely on lots of butter for their flavor as well as characteristics such as crispness, chewiness or melt-in-your-mouth texture, so creating a low-fat cookie can be a challenge. Fat coats the proteins in flour, inhibiting the formation of gluten and thus tenderizing the crumb. It also keeps cookies moist and helps them last longer. You can no more omit the butter or oil in a cookie recipe than you can omit the flour. And the truth is, we all need some fat in our diets, so I'm a strong believer in low-fat rather than fat-free. Besides, remove all the fat from a cookie and you have a cracker.

Our concern should be with both the quantity and quality of fat, that is, how much and what kind. To put it simply, fats are either saturated (bad) or mono- or poly-unsaturated (good). Healthy mono- and poly-unsaturated fats such as canola and olive oil and the fat in nuts and avocados should be included as a regular part of our diets, as they go a long way to prevent coronary heart disease. Trans fats — produced during the hydrogenation process that transforms an otherwise healthy liquid fat into a solid fat such as stick margarine — are particularly harmful and should be avoided entirely. If you're concerned about calories, because fat contains more than twice as many (9 per gram) as protein or carbohydrates (4 per gram), cutting back on fat is also the best way to trim calories.

As a general rule, saturated fats — such as butter, hydrogenated margarine, shortening and animal fats (such as those in beef or bacon) — are solid at room temperature, and unsaturated fats — such as oils (including those in nuts) — are liquid at room temperature. However, solid fats are often necessary in baking, so butter and oil aren't always interchangeable. In my opinion, butter is better and adds essential buttery flavor to cookies, so I typically use ¼ cup in a cookie recipe — proof that a little fat goes a long way!

One of the most important things I learned from years of owning a low-fat cookie bakery and experimenting with various recipes is that most cookie recipes contain far more fat than they need. Another major discovery was that when you remove something from a recipe (such as fat or sugar), you don't always need to replace it with something else. For example, the chocolate chip cookie recipe on the back of the chocolate chips

bag can be made using half the butter called for, with no other alterations, and come out just fine.

Because cookies vary so much in texture—there are chewy cookies, crispy cookies, melt-in-your-mouth cookies—the fat-reducing techniques you use will depend on the type and flavor of cookie you're making and the texture you're going for. There's no magic formula or secret ingredient I use to "replace" the fat in a recipe: usually it's a matter of trial and error. What works in a drop cookie won't necessarily work in a rolled cookie, but might work in a brownie. This is a daunting task for most, and who really wants to waste the time and ingredients to experiment? If you'd like to trim the fat from your own recipes, here are a few tips:

* Applesauce and other fruit purées are popular fat substitutes and can often be used to replace up to 75% of the fat in a recipe, but are better suited to cakes, muffins, quick breads and recipes that call for oil (a liquid) rather than butter or shortening (a solid). Because fruit purées are liquid they tend to produce a cakey texture undesirable in crisp or chewy cookies.

* Try substituting lower-fat (not fat-free) versions of ingredients such as peanut butter, cream cheese, sweetened condensed milk and sour cream.

* Omitting egg yolks is a matter of choice. Each large egg yolk contains 5 grams of fat, but only 1 gram is saturated. Sometimes leaving them in enables you to trim a tablespoon of butter (11 grams) or oil (14 grams) elsewhere in the recipe, and yolks naturally contain lecithin, an ingredient commonly added to prolong the shelf life of baked goods.

* Using more vanilla (2–3 tsp instead of the usual 1 tsp) will help with the flavor and also add a little more moisture.

* If you need to replace some moisture lost by reducing the fat, try increasing

the quantity of other moist ingredients such as molasses or marmalade, and cutting back on the sugar accordingly. Or use brown sugar instead of white, which is no healthier but is moister, as it contains some molasses.

* Cocoa is a great choice to use instead of unsweetened or even semi-sweet baking chocolate. The usual formula is 3 Tbsp cocoa and 1 Tbsp butter or oil to replace 1 square (1 oz) baking chocolate, but you can cut the fat down to a teaspoon, or often eliminate it altogether.

* To begin, try reducing the fat in your original recipe a bit at a time. Usually there's simply more than you need. Then make changes gradually. Don't try everything at once.

* Measure your flour carefully, by stirring it to aerate it and then spooning it into the measuring cup and leveling it off with a knife. When flour gets packed down in its bag or canister, and you scoop it out, you could add up to ¼ cup too much flour per cup that you scoop, which could make your dough dry, particularly when you use less fat.

* Remember not to overmix or overbake your dough.

Now you're on your way to making a great lower-fat cookie!

Fat & All That

by Guido Van Rosendaal, M.D.

Wouldn't it be nice to enjoy desserts and snacks and not worry that they may not be good for you? It's actually quite easy to improve your nutrition and reduce your calories while maintaining, and often improving, the flavors of your favorite foods. Here's the skinny on food and nutrition, to help you understand the science behind this book.

About food & eating

The foods we eat contain energy, and they differ in the forms that energy takes. We need this energy — mostly in the form of fats and carbohydrates — to fuel our bodies for growth and daily activity. If we take in more energy than we need, our bodies store it, partly as a quick energy source, but also as long-term storage — fat.

Unfortunately, our early ancestors often had too little food for long periods of time, so they developed a constitution that drove them to seek out extra calories to store for "rainy days." This appetite for food is ingrained in our genes, and because of this genetic makeup we're not very good at shutting down our energy-seeking behavior when our calorie stores are adequate. Add to this the fact that we now have easy access to large quantities of good-tasting food and we have a problem! It's easy to take in more energy than we need.

What our food is made of

Simple sugars provide a sweet taste and are the basic building blocks from which carbohydrates are made. In many foods these sugar molecules are linked to each other in chains that require digesting before our bodies can use them. These foods are called complex carbohydrates. The glucose we eat as table sugar requires no digestion and enters the blood stream very quickly compared to chains of glucose in the form of starch. The starch in potatoes or flour, for example, is made from the same sugar, doesn't taste sweet but requires digestion in the intestinal tract to gradually release this sugar. Carbohydrate chains not easily digested for energy are called fiber. Fiber is found in vegetables, fruits and whole grains.

As our bodies grow and continually rebuild and repair, we need proteins, the building blocks for our bodies that are also essential for many of the body's functions. The building blocks from which proteins are made are amino acids. We need to eat proteins to create new tissue and for the constant repair and replacement that our bodies undergo. High quality or complete proteins — ones that contain all the amino acids our bodies need — can be found in milk, egg whites, beans, soy, fish and meat. When we take in more protein than we need to build and renew our body structure, we use the extra for energy.

Fats are a concentrated energy source with a texture and flavor we crave — thanks to our genes! They make foods taste especially good, but weight for weight they deliver almost twice as many calories as the same amount of carbohydrate or protein. Importantly, not all fats are created equal. Some provide health benefits, while others—some of which are plentiful in baked goods—are harmful.

Cholesterol & all that

Consuming too many calories and eating the wrong foods will increase your risk of several health problems, including diabetes, some cancers and atherosclerosis. Atherosclerosis is the accumulation of cholesterol on the walls of our arteries, and it affects our health by reducing circulation to one part of the body or other. Some of its effects are serious. Heart attacks and strokes, for instance, disable or kill many people each year.

Atherosclerosis affects us all to some degree and progresses as we age. The amount of fat deposited in our arteries varies from person to person and to some extent is out of our control. If we've inherited high-risk genes we'll have more severe atherosclerosis at an earlier age than our friends or neighbors who don't have these genes. In women, the rate of progression of atherosclerosis increases after menopause. For each of us, regardless of those factors over which we have no control, the rate at which we deposit cholesterol in our arteries depends on what we eat. It is, therefore, very important for us to develop eating habits to reduce this risk and so maximize our health and life expectancy.

The narrowing of our arteries progresses when we consume too many calories, particularly in the form of certain fats. Saturated and "trans" fats are the worst of these. Saturated fats are found in red meat, butter, lard, cheese, cream, shortening, palm and coconut oil. Polyunsaturated fats, particularly vegetable oils, such as canola, are much healthier, although they still have the disadvantage of providing far more calories, weight for weight, compared to carbohydrates or proteins. Unfortunately, when such oils are "hydrogenated" their health benefits are lost, partly because trans fats are produced, which are at least as unhealthy as saturated fats. Trans fats are found in deep-fried fast foods, bakery products, packaged snack foods, margarines and crackers.

Monounsaturated fats, such as those in olive and canola oil, can help to prevent atherosclerosis when they replace saturated fats in your diet. It's best to use polyunsaturated or monounsaturated fats instead of saturated or trans fats whenever possible and in general to reduce the fat we consume.

Our bodies produce most of the cholesterol that circulates in our blood and ends up clogging our arteries. The more excess fuel we ingest, particularly as saturated or trans fats, the more atherosclerosis we'll develop. The cholesterol in our food also adds to this, so we should minimize eating foods that contain lots of it, such as egg yolks.

About sugar

Our bodies easily and quickly absorb sugar. It doesn't need to be digested and enters directly into the bloodstream. This uptake is the same for table sugar, fruit juice concentrate or honey. The result is a surge in blood sugar to which the body reacts by pumping large amounts of insulin into the blood stream to reduce the sugar level.

This rapid uptake of simple sugars has two undesirable effects. First, the resulting insulin surge may lower blood sugar to a level lower than normal, which in turn may produce hunger shortly after we've eaten. Second, the high sugar and insulin levels will have a negative effect on the body's metabolism, hastening the depositing of cholesterol on the walls of our arteries. When we eat carbohydrates in their complex form, absorption is delayed because of the time needed for digestion. Sugar enters the blood stream more slowly, and the rise in blood sugar is lower.

Ideally our carbohydrate intake should include as much indigestible fiber as possible. Also, if we mix our refined sugars with fats and proteins, as with a meal, their absorption will be delayed because they'll be emptied from the stomach more slowly and sugar absorption will take longer, resulting in lower levels of both blood sugar and insulin.

What about low carbohydrate diets?

While some people can reduce their weight with these diets, there are potential long-term negative effects. Eating a low carbohydrate, high protein diet means eating lots of fat, and much of this will unavoidably be saturated or trans fats. Carbohydrates are essential to a balanced diet, but they should be eaten as much as possible in their complex form and only in moderation as highly refined "simple" sugars. Balance is the key!

Some general nutritional strategies:

1 Minimize the amount of fat you eat, especially saturated or trans fats.

2 Whenever possible, replace saturated or trans fats with complex carbohydrates, especially those with lots of fiber (fruits, whole grains), protein (egg whites, skim milk powder), fats that are unsaturated or monounsaturated (olive oil, canola oil) or foods that contain combinations of such nutrients (yogurt, nuts).

3 Eat simple sugars in moderation, except when you exercise vigorously, and replace simple sugars with complex carbohydrates whenever possible.

4 If you eat foods with a high sugar content and don't need a quick energy source, add these to a meal that contains fats, proteins and complex carbohydrates to reduce the effect on your blood sugar level.

5 Avoid foods with trans fats.

6 Eat a balanced diet of foods you enjoy, prepared with the healthiest ingredients available.

Cookie Baking Techniques

Measuring

When measuring your ingredients, you need to understand the difference between dry and liquid measuring cups. Dry measuring cups are metal or plastic. But liquids are measured in glass or plastic cups with the measures marked on the side. To measure liquid in a liquid cup, always read the measurement at eye level while the cup is on a flat surface.

You can also measure liquids in dry cups, but dry ingredients can't be measured in liquid measuring cups. If you measure a dry ingredient such as flour in a liquid cup, you'll end up with an inaccurate amount. To read the numbers on the side of the cup, you'll have to pack down the flour, which will usually give you too much. To measure flour, fill the measuring cup with as little flour as possible. The best way to do this is to stir the flour to aerate it (fluff it up), then gently scoop or spoon the flour into the measuring cup and level the top with a knife or other flat edge. Brown sugar is another matter: to measure it, make sure it's packed, unless otherwise specified.

Mixing

One of the most important rules for baking low-fat cookies is don't overmix! Certain ingredients are sometimes beaten well on purpose — for example, to aerate (incorporate air into) the butter and sugar, or to whip egg whites. However, gently fold dry ingredients into the wet, just until they're combined. Otherwise the gluten in the flour will develop into strands, and you'll end up with tough cookies. This is why butter, sugar, eggs and other ingredients are beaten together first, and the dry ingredients are blended and then stirred in by hand — so that the two are combined with a minimum number of strokes, to avoid overmixing. This technique is often referred to as "the quick bread method," because it's used when making muffins and quick breads.

Dropping & Shaping

To bake a batch of dropped or shaped cookies, make sure they're all roughly the same size (or with rolled or icebox cookies, the same thickness), so that they'll bake evenly. I usually use a heaping teaspoon (not the measuring kind) to drop cookie dough onto a sheet, or roll it into walnut-sized balls. Make them smaller or larger if you like, but adjust your baking time accordingly, and watch carefully during the last few minutes of baking to ensure they don't end up overbaked and dry.

Drop cookies should be spaced about 2 inches apart on a cookie sheet, including the space between the cookies and the edge of the sheet, unless otherwise specified in the recipe. Rolled, shaped and icebox cookies usually don't spread as much, so you can get away with placing them closer together — 1 inch apart is usually fine. If you're not sure, bake the first batch with extra room in between them so they don't run together. Never put cookie dough onto a hot cookie sheet, as it'll start to melt and spread too quickly.

Cookie Sheets & Baking Pans

For the best results, choose cookie sheets made from shiny heavyweight aluminum, with low sides or a lip on one edge. Dark sheets tend to absorb heat, making cookies brown too fast and burn on the bottom. I don't like using insulated cookie sheets, as the cookies don't bake properly on the bottom and often spread too much, not to mention the sheets are difficult to clean without getting water inside their seams. (I once had one puff up like a balloon in the oven when the bit of moisture that had leaked inside turned to steam!) However, if the bottoms of your cookies burn, make your own insulated sheet by doubling up your cookie sheets with a few pennies between them to create a pocket of air.

Make sure your cookie sheets are at least 2 inches smaller than your oven on all sides so that the air can properly circulate. To bake brownies and squares, always use the pan size specified in the recipe. Using a larger pan will mean your batter is spread too thin and will cook too quickly; a smaller pan will make your batter too thick and it won't cook through properly. If you're using a glass baking dish, reduce your oven temperature by 25°F, as glass retains heat more efficiently than aluminum.

Baking

The second most important rule for low-fat cookies is not to overbake them, particularly when you want them to be chewy. (Do you remember the first rule? Don't overmix the dough! I can't emphasize this enough.) Overbaking makes cookies dry, and low-fat cookies are even more susceptible to drying out, so watch your baking time carefully. Low-fat cookies, particularly chewy cookies and brownies, are almost always best when just barely done, almost underdone. Keep in mind they'll continue to cook a bit after they come out of the oven — particularly brownies, which must cool in the pan. All cookies will firm up as they cool, so if they're set all the way through when they come out of the oven, they won't be chewy once they've cooled completely. Chocolate chip cookies, for example, should be pale golden around the edges only (not all the way through), and set around the edges but still soft in the middle.

The rules for rolled cookies and icebox cookies are a little different. They can be made crisper, if you like them that way, by cooking them a little longer or rolling or slicing them thinner. Of course biscotti are double baked, so they're hard to overbake. An extended baking time will only make them harder and drier. With any kind of cookie, check for doneness at the earliest suggested baking time, keeping in mind that oven temperatures vary. If you think your oven is too hot or too cool, buy an oven thermometer (available at kitchenware and department stores for around $5), and check to see if your oven temperature is accurate. If it isn't, you don't need to get your oven calibrated, just adjust the temperature accordingly. Always make sure the rack is in the middle of the oven, and bake only one sheet of cookies at a time to ensure even baking.

Storing

Low-fat baked goods don't stay fresh as long as those that are high in fat, so always ensure your cookies are properly stored. If you aren't going to eat them in a day or two, tightly wrap and freeze them. Always make sure cookies are completely cool before storing.

Soft cookies should be stored in an airtight container. If they're frosted, let the frosting set before storing in a single layer. Crisp cookies should be stored in a loosely covered container, such as a cookie jar, unless you live in a humid climate.

Never store crisp and soft cookies together. The crisp cookies will absorb the moisture from the soft ones, making them soft and the soft ones drier. In fact, different types of cookies shouldn't be stored together at all, or they'll pick up each others' flavors. To freeze, place waxed paper between the layers and wrap well in plastic wrap or store in a zip-lock freezer bag or well-sealed container.

Troubleshooting

Cookies are spreading too much
Your oven may be too cool, causing the dough to melt before it has a chance to set; try increasing the oven temperature. Chilling the dough before baking will also cause the cookies to spread more slowly as they bake. And remember — never put cookie dough on hot cookie sheets.

Cookies aren't spreading enough
Your oven may be too hot, causing the cookies to set on the outside before they can spread out; decrease the oven temperature.

Cookies are baking unevenly
Your oven could have hot spots. Try rotating your cookie sheet halfway through baking, and make sure your cookies are the same size.

Tough cookies
You may have overmixed your dough after the flour was added to the wet ingredients. Once you add the dry ingredients to the wet, fold them together gently, just until they're combined.

Dry cookie dough
You may have added too much flour. When it's scooped directly out of its canister, flour is often packed down, which means you could be adding up to ¼ cup too much flour per cup that you scoop. Stir it up to aerate it, then gently scoop or spoon into a measuring cup and level off with a knife.

About Your Ingredients

Fats

Fats add tenderness, texture, flavor and moistness, all important characteristics of a good cookie, brownie or square. How rich a cookie tastes depends mostly on the type of fat it contains and how it was incorporated into the batter. But not all fats are created equal! Not only do different fats have drastically different flavors and nutritional values, the difference in consistency between butter and oil will make a huge difference in the texture and structure of your cookie. Since oil is a liquid and butter (or shortening or stick margarine) is solid, they can't be used interchangeably when baking without affecting a recipe.

Using butter in your cookies adds a wonderful flavor that can't be duplicated with oil or shortening. Butter is often the ingredient that makes a low-fat cookie taste as good and as satisfying as its high-fat counterpart. Butter's low melting point makes cookies soft on the inside, crisp and golden on the outside. If you choose to use margarine, use non-hydrogenated margarine, which doesn't contain harmful trans fats, but remember that tub margarines have a higher water content, which sometimes make cookies cakier in texture.

Whipped butter, diet spreads and butter blends are made by whipping fillers such as water, yogurt or even air into regular or skim-milk products and should be avoided at all costs when baking. Save these for spreading on your toast.

If you're going to use oil, canola is the best choice, both nutritionally and because of its neutral flavor. It's extremely low in saturated fat and high in healthy monounsaturated fats as well as linolenic acid, the plant version of omega-3 fatty acids. Nut oils can also be used instead of canola oil, and generally add a nutty flavor to cookies, which works. Olive oil is a great choice for cooking, but virgin olive oils are stronger in flavor and generally don't suit cookies. Shortening is 100% fat and isn't as sensitive to temperature changes as butter or margarine; some bakers use shortening in their cookies so that they won't spread as much and are more consistent. Because shortening adds absolutely no flavor or nutritional benefits, it isn't used in this book.

Fat Replacers

Applesauce and other fruit purées are popular fat substitutes and can often be used to replace up to 75% of the fat in a recipe, but are better suited to cakes, muffins and quick breads—baked goods that have a cakey texture. Prune purée is a common choice because prunes are high in fiber, largely in the form of pectin. Pectin helps to entrap air during the creaming process, and coats the proteins in flour the way fat does, and so inhibits the formation of tough strands of gluten. If you want to give prune purée a try, buy a jar of baby food prunes, or to make your own: purée 1½ cups of prunes with ½ cup hot water in a food processor. Store in a sealed container in the fridge. Other good choices are mashed banana, canned pumpkin and puréed drained canned pears or peaches.

Flour & Grains

Flour gives your cookies structure, and also boosts fiber. There are many different kinds of flour, but wheat flour is the kind most often used for baking. Other types of flour such as rice or barley flour don't have the same gluten content as wheat flour, so substituting them will often result in a gooey mess.

There's a wide range of wheat flour available. It's easy to decide what type you should choose if you understand the difference between them. All the recipes in this book were developed using all-purpose flour. Bleached and unbleached will work equally well in your recipe. Bleached flour differs only in that it has been made whiter. Any lost nutrients are generally replaced, but I prefer to use unbleached flour.

The basic difference between bread, cake, pastry and all-purpose flour is the protein content. When you add a liquid to flour and stir, two proteins, glutelin and gliadin, grab the water and each other to form stretchy, elastic sheets of gluten. If the flour you choose is high in these proteins, it absorbs a lot of water and makes lots of tough, springy gluten. High-protein flour such as bread flour is essential for baking yeast breads,

because such loaves require gluten for their structure. Cookies, cakes and quick breads, on the other hand, require a more tender texture.

All-purpose flour is used in a wide range of baked goods, but because it's multi-purpose, its protein content can vary greatly depending on the brand and where it was milled. This is why so many cooks have a favorite brand they stick with for years. Self-rising flour has had baking powder and salt added, and can't be used interchangeably with all-purpose flour. Low protein cake and pastry flour is chlorinated, and because fat sticks to chlorinated starch, it also helps to evenly distribute the air bubbles and gives a velvety texture. It's generally a good choice for baking low-fat cookies, but isn't necessary for a recipe's success.

Whole wheat flour has been milled from the entire kernel of wheat, so it contains the bran and wheat germ. If you want to boost fiber in your cookie recipe, try replacing up to half of the all-purpose flour with whole wheat flour, keeping in mind that your cookies will be slightly darker and heavier. Replacing all the flour with whole wheat flour often results in a heavy cookie with a gummy texture. Whole wheat pastry flour has a finer texture, and works well if you can find it.

Store flour in an airtight container in a cool, dry place for up to 15 months, or in the freezer for up to 2 years. The oils in whole wheat flour can become rancid, so it's best stored in the refrigerator or freezer.

Oats

Oats are an excellent addition to any diet. They're packed with complex carbohydrates and soluble fiber, which can lower blood cholesterol and keep hunger at bay by making you feel full longer. They're low in fat, and most of the fat they contain is polyunsaturated. Oats are an excellent source of protein, and are rich in iron, the B-complex vitamins, vitamin E and zinc. They're also high in calcium, potassium and magnesium.

When baking cookies with oats, rolled, old-fashioned and quick-cooking oats (NOT steel-cut or instant) can be used interchangeably unless specified in a recipe. What's the difference? Rolled or old-fashioned oats are steamed, then flattened into flakes. Because they're bigger, they impart a more rugged texture and don't absorb as much moisture. Quick-cooking oats are cut into pieces before being steamed and flattened. They

have a more tender texture and because they're smaller, they absorb moisture better. Instant oats are cut into very small pieces, then precooked and dried. Neither instant (too pasty) nor steel-cut (they're cut whole grains) oats should be used for baking, unless specified in a recipe.

Like nuts, oats can be toasted to boost flavor and add a little crunch. Spread oats in a dry pan and cook over medium heat, shaking the pan often, just until the oats begin to turn golden and fragrant. You can toast oats before using them in any recipe. Oats can also be ground to a fine powder and used to replace a small amount (up to one quarter) of flour in a recipe. This will boost fiber as well as nutritional value, and add a slightly nutty flavor, especially if the oats are toasted. Place 1¼ cups of old-fashioned or quick-cooking oats in a blender or food processor and blend for about a minute to get 1 cup of ground oats.

Sweeteners

Sugar does more than sweeten baked goods. It aids in browning and tenderizes by preventing the proteins in flour from joining and forming gluten, which is important when you're reducing the other tenderizing ingredient: fat. But is sugar as bad for you as fat? If you're concerned about calories, sugar has just 4 calories per gram, compared to the 9 calories found in a gram of fat.

Despite common belief, unless you're diabetic there's no difference to your body between table sugar and sugar in any other form, such as "less refined" molasses or honey. That is, there are no caloric or nutritional benefits to sweetening your cookies with honey or concentrated fruit juice rather than with granulated sugar. Products labeled "sweetened with fruit juice" sound healthier, but when fruit juice is concentrated and used as a sweetener its nutritional components are stripped away and you're left with just sugar.

Granulated white sugar is refined, meaning 99% of the impurities and nutrients are extracted. It adds sweetness, tenderness and moisture, and helps a cookie to brown and spread. Cookies with a higher ratio of sugar to flour will be more tender and crisper around the edges.

Brown sugar is white sugar that has had some molasses left in it or added to it. Light and dark brown sugars can generally be used interchangeably. The only difference is that dark brown sugar contains more molasses. Brown sugar adds sweetness, moisture and a caramel-like flavor, which comes in handy when reducing the fat in a cookie. To measure brown sugar, always pack it firmly, unless otherwise specified in the recipe. To soften brown sugar quickly, place it in a microwave-safe dish, add a soft piece of bread or wedge of apple, cover tightly and microwave for 30 seconds.

Icing sugar — also known as powdered or confectioner's sugar — is white sugar that's been ground to a powder and had a little cornstarch added to prevent clumping. Because it dissolves more easily it's most often used in frostings, but it often helps give cookies a fine crumb and tender texture. Icing sugar can't be used interchangeably with granulated sugar.

Honey adds a unique flavor and contains some nutrients, but in such small quantities they aren't beneficial. Honey acts as a humectant, meaning it attracts moisture from the air, so cookies and bars made with honey will be soft and may become gummy when stored. Since it's a liquid, honey can easily throw a recipe off balance if used instead of sugar. It's also much sweeter than sugar, so you don't need to use as much. To liquefy creamed or crystallized honey, simply warm it on the stove or in the microwave.

Molasses is a by-product of sugar refining. It's what's left over after the granulated sugar has been extracted from the sugar cane. It's available in light and dark varieties, and provides more nutrients than any other sweetener, but still in very small quantities for the amount used in baking. I generally use dark molasses for its rich color and deeper flavor, but the two can be substituted for each other.

Corn syrup is made by converting the starch of corn kernels into sugar. Like honey and molasses, syrup adds moistness to baked goods, and will make them brown more quickly. Dark and light corn syrup can be used interchangeably, unless otherwise specified in a recipe. Although dark corn syrup has some added caramel flavoring, corn syrup doesn't add a distinct flavor as honey and molasses do.

Maple syrup is boiled down from maple sap. Although it's more expensive than other sweeteners, it adds a deliciously unique flavor to baked goods and frostings, and less expensive grade B syrup is fine for baking. Keep in mind it's more liquid than honey, molasses or corn syrups, and should be kept in the fridge, or it will go moldy. It may darken, but that won't affect the flavor.

Eggs

If you're worried about your fat intake, you'll be happy to know that 1 large egg contains only 5 grams of fat, and of those 5 grams, only 1 gram is saturated. All the fat in an egg is in its yolk. Eggs are one of the best food sources of vitamin D (second only to fish liver oil), and a great source of vitamins A and E. Eggs also contain folate, iron and most of the B vitamins. In cookie baking, eggs have a binding effect, and create a smooth, compact texture as well as richness, moisture and even provide some leavening.

Always use large eggs when following a recipe. Almost all recipes are based on large eggs, which are regulated to ensure they're 2 ounces in the shell. Since an egg is a liquid, using extra-large or medium eggs could throw a recipe off balance, but it's better to go bigger than smaller.

Because all the fat is in the yolk, a common fat-reducing technique is to replace all of the eggs in a recipe with egg whites. However, using too many egg whites can result in rubbery cookies. Because egg yolks contain only 5 grams of fat and naturally contain lecithin — an ingredient commonly added as a preservative to increase the shelf life of baked goods — I often keep a whole egg in my recipes, which allows me to reduce the butter or oil even further. If you're experimenting with a recipe that contains more than two eggs, try substituting just one or two of them with whites.

To beat egg whites, always use a clean glass or stainless steel bowl, but it doesn't matter whether the eggs are chilled or at room temperature. For properly beaten egg whites, foamy means they're shiny with large and small bubbles; soft peaks means the eggs stand in soft peaks when the beater is withdrawn, and they slide around as one mass, not sticking to the sides of the bowl. Stiff peaks means the peaks stand straight up on their own, and the egg doesn't slide around in the bowl anymore. If you've gone too far and overbeaten your egg whites (overbeaten whites look like a stiff, dry mass), simply add another egg white for every 3 to 4 overbeaten whites and beat for about 30 seconds.

Dairy Products

Buttermilk is low-fat or skim milk to which a bacterial culture has been added, making it very thick, creamy and tangy, yet low in fat. It falls in between skim and 1% milk in fat content. About 20% of its calories come from fat. If you don't have buttermilk, you can substitute thin yogurt or sour milk. To make sour milk, put 1 Tbsp lemon juice or vinegar in a measuring cup and fill with milk to make 1 cup. Stir and let sit for 5 minutes before using.

Sweetened condensed milk is a thick canned sweetened milk that has had about 50% of its water removed. The reduced fat varieties are just as good as the regular and add rich creaminess to low-fat recipes, but note that they contain almost as many calories.

Evaporated milk is canned milk that has had about 60% of its water removed. Don't mistake it for sweetened condensed milk. Although it's richer than regular milk, it isn't sweetened and isn't as thick. Evaporated milk adds richness to recipes that call for whole milk or cream.

Low-fat or fat-free yogurt and sour cream are great alternatives to the full-fat varieties. If you find a low-fat yogurt too runny, strain it for an hour or so in a double layer of cheesecloth set over a bowl. The longer you strain it, the thicker it'll get.

Reduced fat cream cheese is an excellent substitute for regular cream cheese in cheesecake brownies and squares, as well as some kinds of cookie dough. It has a much better flavor and mouth feel than fat-free varieties, which tend to be grainy and flavorless.

Leavening Agents

Baking soda and baking powder are chemical leavening agents that produce carbon dioxide gas, just as yeast does. When you add it to your cookie batter, baking soda creates a carbon dioxide gas (bubbles) as it comes in contact with moisture and an acid, such as brown sugar, buttermilk, chocolate, molasses or fruit juice. Because less acidic dough browns better, baking soda is often added to an acidic dough as a neutralizer rather than as a leavener, to create good browning. Since baking soda begins to work right away, it's best to work quickly and not let the batter sit for long, as the soda will lose its punch.

Double-acting baking powder doesn't need to react to an acidic ingredient, as it's made up of baking soda and just enough acid to produce its own leavening power. It works in two stages, reacting first to moisture and then again to heat from the oven. Cookies made with baking powder spread less, rise higher, bake more quickly and don't brown as well. When a recipe calls for both, the soda neutralizes the acid and contributes to the browning, while the powder does the leavening. Don't dip a wet spoon into the baking powder container or you'll deactivate the whole batch.

Salt

Salt is important because it enhances the flavors of the other ingredients. If you're concerned about your salt intake, reduce the amount rather than omitting it altogether. Baked goods with no salt will taste flat.

Chocolate & Cocoa

Chocolate in its many forms has always been a favorite addition to cookies, brownies and squares. Luckily, chocolate isn't as unhealthy as you might think. The saturated fat in chocolate is mostly in the form of stearic acid, a type of fat that doesn't increase LDL (bad) cholesterol in the blood, and may even improve it. Chocolate also contains potent antioxidants like those found in red wine. Chocolate in all its forms is

derived from cacao beans, which have been roasted, hulled and ground to make chocolate liquor. Dark, semi-sweet, bittersweet and milk chocolates differ in flavor and texture because they contain different ratios of chocolate liquor to cocoa butter and sugar. Milk chocolate also contains milk or cream.

Although cocoa butter is what gives white chocolate its chocolate flavor, it's often not considered actual chocolate because it contains no chocolate liquor. Sugar, milk solids, vanilla and lecithin are added to the cocoa butter to make white chocolate. Nutritionally, the darker the chocolate is, the better; semi-sweet and bittersweet chocolate can be used interchangeably in a recipe.

Stored in a cool, dry place, most chocolate will last up to 2 years. It won't keep any longer if stored in the fridge, and will often pick up odors or bloom, a greyish white film that appears on the surface of chocolate exposed to extreme temperature variations. Bloom won't affect the flavor or quality of chocolate, and will disappear upon baking or melting.

Because it burns easily, chocolate must be melted slowly and gently over low heat. The best way is in a double boiler set over very hot water. Chop the chocolate into pieces first to make it melt more quickly and evenly. When melted in the microwave, most chocolate (except unsweetened) will become shiny but not change its shape until it's stirred. Don't worry about small lumps that remain — they'll melt with stirring.

Even the smallest amount of moisture will cause melted chocolate to seize, and suddenly become very thick and lumpy. If this happens, add about a teaspoon of butter or oil for every 2 ounces of chocolate, and gently stir until melted and smooth. To avoid seizing, make sure all your bowls, saucepans and utensils are completely dry before using.

Cocoa powder is made when chocolate liquor is pressed to remove half to three quarters of the cocoa butter (fat), and then dried. It's the best choice if you're trying to reduce fat, and it often produces richer, more chocolatey baked goods. One ounce of unsweetened chocolate contains 16 grams of fat, compared to the 1.5 grams of fat in 3 Tbsp (an equal amount, flavor-wise) of cocoa.

There are two kinds of cocoa powder: Dutch process (also called European style) is treated with alkali to neutralize its naturally acidic taste, making it darker and smoother, with a more intense flavor. American style is non-alkalized and lighter in color. Although they can be used interchangeably, I recommend using Dutch process cocoa because of its deep color, rich flavor and smooth texture. Always use high-quality cocoa for best results. Stored in a tightly covered container in a cool, dry place, cocoa will keep indefinitely.

Chocolate syrup is often overlooked as a low-fat ingredient, but I often use it in cookies, brownies and cakes for its sweetness and deep chocolate flavor. Be sure you know the difference between chocolate syrup, which contains only cocoa or chocolate liquor, sugar, water and other flavorings, and chocolate fudge topping, which usually contains milk, cream or butter and isn't low in fat.

A word about carob. If you think that carob might be a wise alternative to chocolate, it isn't! Although it's caffeine-free, carob contains more saturated fat than chocolate, just as much sugar, not as much flavor and none of the helpful antioxidants.

Nuts

Although all varieties of nuts are high in fat and calories, nutritionally they make an excellent addition to any cookie. The fat in nuts is almost all unsaturated, and they're rich in omega-3 fatty acids, known for their positive protective effect against blood cholesterol. Almost all nuts also contain linolenic acid, which counteracts cholesterol and protects against heart disease. A recent study found that those who consumed nuts at least five times a week (2 ounces a day) had a significantly lower risk of developing heart disease. Nuts are also an excellent source of protein and fiber, and they contain important nutrients such as folic acid, vitamin B2, vitamin B6, iron, zinc, potassium and copper.

If you're trying to limit your calories, use the amount called for in a recipe. If you're more concerned with a healthy diet, don't be afraid to add more nuts than these recipes call for, or throw a handful into a cookie batter.

Nuts can easily become rancid, so they're best bought in small quantities and/or stored tightly covered in your refrigerator. Frozen, they'll last up to 2 years.

Toasting nuts maximizes their flavor as well as their crunch. To toast nuts, spread in an even layer in a dry frying pan. Toast over medium heat on the stovetop, shaking the pan frequently, just until golden and fragrant, about 6 to 8 minutes. Watch carefully so that they don't burn; once they begin to turn golden, they darken very quickly, and there's nothing you can do to salvage burnt nuts. To chop or grind nuts in a food processor, add a few spoonfuls of sugar from your recipe to keep the nuts from turning into nut butter. Keep batches small and pulse until they're the consistency you're after.

Dried Fruit

Dried fruit is the perfect choice if you want to add something sweet and chewy to your cookies. They're an excellent source of all kinds of vitamins, minerals and fiber. Chopped dried fruits are generally interchangeable in a recipe, so don't be afraid to experiment, but no matter what type of dried fruit you

use, make sure it's nice and plump. Too-dried-out fruit will absorb moisture from your dough or batter, drying it out. To plump it up, cover with hot water or other liquid, let soak for at least 10 minutes, and drain well before using.

Raisins are rich in iron, calcium, potassium, magnesium and phosphorus as well as the B vitamins and some vitamin A. Dried cranberries are high in fiber and vitamin C, and are also a great source of heart-healthy bioflavonoids. Dried apricots are one of the healthiest foods you can eat. They're rich in fiber, iron, potassium and riboflavin, and are loaded with beta carotene.

Other Cookie Additions

The oil in coconut has a higher concentration of saturated fat than any other food, and 80% of the calories in coconut come from fat. The recipes in this book with coconut call for only a small amount, usually made up for with larger quantities of dried fruit, nuts or oats. By all means omit it, if you like.

As with nuts and oats, coconut can be toasted to boost flavor and add crunch. Toast in a dry frying pan over medium heat, stirring frequently, for 5–7 minutes or until golden and fragrant. To add coconut flavor without adding any fat, try coconut extract.

Flaxseed has just recently become more widely recognized in North America for its amazing health benefits. Besides being rich in iron, niacin, potassium,

phosphorous and vitamin E, flaxseed is high in fiber, has 75 times more antioxidants than broccoli, and 6 times the phytoestrogens of soy. Because the body can't digest whole flaxseeds, it's best to grind them first. Use a coffee or spice mill and keep leftovers in a sealed container in the fridge for up to a month. A couple of spoonfuls of ground flax are almost undetectable sprinkled into most cookie doughs (particularly those with a grainy texture), or a graham crumb crust.

Coffee is often added to chocolate-based recipes (such as brownies) to deepen the chocolate flavor without adding fat or calories. Make a coffee extract by dissolving a teaspoon of instant coffee powder into a teaspoon of water, and add it along with (or instead of) the vanilla in a recipe. Don't worry about your cookies tasting like coffee; unless you add a large amount, they won't.

Oatmeal Raisin Cookies

Chocolate Chip Cookies

Banana Oatmeal Raisin Cookies

Inside-Out Chocolate Chunk Cookies

Triple Chocolate Chunk Cookies

Double Chocolate Apricot Cookies

Monster Cookies

Chocolate Oatmeal Cranberry Cookies

Breakfast Bean Cookies

Almond Butter Chocolate Chip Cookies

Black & White Cookies

Crispy Chocolate Walnut Cookies

Macaroons

Chocolate Pecan Brown Sugar Bundles

Chocolate Bliss

Chocolate Peanut Butter Oat Cookies

Carrot Cake Cookies

Pumpkin Hermits

Fresh Apple & Cheddar Hermits

Grandma Woodall's Marmalade Cookies

Drop Cookies

Ingredients

¼ cup butter or non-hydrogenated margarine, softened
1½ cups packed brown sugar
2 large eggs
2 tsp vanilla
1½ cups flour
1 cup oats
1 tsp baking soda
1 tsp cinnamon
¼ tsp salt
1 cup raisins

Nutrition Facts

Per cookie

Calories	141
Fat	2.7 g
Saturated	1.4 g
Monounsaturated	0.8 g
Polyunsaturated	0.3 g
Carbohydrates	27.7 g
Cholesterol	23 mg
Protein	2.2 g
Fiber	1 g
Calories from fat	17%

Oatmeal Raisin Cookies

Of course oatmeal-raisin cookies don't have to be made with raisins: try substituting other dried fruit such as cranberries, cherries, chopped apricots or even blueberries. Just make sure the fruit you use is plump. Too-dried-out fruit will draw moisture out of the cookie dough and make your cookies dry. Plump up raisins or other dried fruit by covering with hot water or other liquid; let stand 10 minutes and drain well.

Preheat the oven to 325°F.

In a large bowl, beat the butter, brown sugar, eggs and vanilla until smooth. In a medium bowl, stir together the flour, oats, baking soda, cinnamon and salt. Add the flour mixture to the sugar mixture and stir by hand until almost combined; add the raisins and stir just until blended.

Drop spoonfuls of dough about 2 inches apart on a cookie sheet that has been sprayed with non-stick spray. Bake for 10–12 minutes, until pale golden around the edges but still soft in the middle. Transfer to a wire rack to cool.

Makes 2 dozen cookies.

Oatmeal Chocolate Chip Cookies

Omit the cinnamon and replace raisins with 1 cup chocolate chips. Adds 1.6 g fat per cookie.

Oatmeal Chocolate Chip & Caramel Chunk Cookies

Chop 20 unwrapped square caramels into quarters with oiled scissors or a knife, and add them along with 1 cup chocolate chips, instead of the raisins. Adds 2.3 g fat per cookie.

Cranberry White Chocolate Oatmeal Cookies

Replace the raisins with 1 cup white chocolate chips or chunks and ½ cup dried cranberries. Adds 1.6 g fat per cookie.

Chocolate-Covered Raisin Oatmeal Cookies

Omit the cinnamon and add 1½ cups chocolate-covered raisins instead of the raisins. Adds 1.4 g fat per cookie.

Cranberry Orange Oatmeal Cookies

Add the grated zest of an orange to the brown sugar mixture, omit the cinnamon and replace the raisins with 1 cup dried cranberries. Fat content remains the same.

Chocolate Chip Cookies

These are the Real Thing—chewy and soft, with crispy edges and lots of chocolate chips. They contain less than half the fat of traditional chocolate chip cookies, without sacrificing taste or texture.

The biggest problem people have when trying to make chewy chocolate chip cookies is overbaking; remember that they firm up as they cool, so if they're golden all over and set, they won't be chewy once they cool down. Make sure they're golden and set around the edges, but still very soft in the middle if you want chewy cookies.

Preheat the oven to 350°F.

In a large bowl, beat the butter and brown sugar until well combined. The mixture will have the consistency of wet sand. Add the egg, corn syrup and vanilla and beat until smooth.

Add the flour, baking soda and salt (stir them together first if you want to) to the butter-sugar mixture and stir by hand until almost combined; add the chocolate chips and stir just until blended.

Drop spoonfuls of dough about 2 inches apart on a cookie sheet that has been sprayed with non-stick spray. Bake for 12–15 minutes, or until pale golden and just set around the edges but still soft in the middle. Don't overbake if you want them to be chewy. Transfer to a wire rack to cool.

Makes 20 cookies.

Maple Chocolate Chip Cookies

Substitute maple syrup for the corn syrup, and maple extract for the vanilla. These are great with chocolate, white chocolate or butterscotch chips, and the nutritional value remains the same.

Ingredients

¼ cup butter or non-hydroge-
    nated margarine, softened
1 cup packed brown sugar
1 large egg
2 Tbsp corn syrup
2 tsp vanilla
1½ cups all-purpose flour
1 tsp baking soda
¼ tsp salt
¾ cup chocolate chips

Nutrition Facts

Per cookie

Calories	155
Fat	5 g
Saturated	3 g
Monounsaturated	1.4 g
Polyunsaturated	0.5 g
Carbohydrates	25.5 g
Cholesterol	17.6 mg
Protein	2 g
Fiber	1 g
Calories from fat	29%

CLOCKWISE FROM RIGHT: Peanut Butter Cookies p. 62; Chocolate Chip Cookies p. 36; Grandma Woodall's Marmalade Cookies p. 55

Ingredients

¼ cup butter or non-hydrogenated margarine, softened
½ cup sugar
½ cup packed brown sugar
1 cup mashed ripe banana
   (about 2 bananas)
1 large egg
2 tsp vanilla
2 cups oats
½ cup all-purpose flour
½ cup whole wheat flour
½ tsp baking soda
¼ tsp cinnamon
¼ tsp salt
1 cup raisins

Nutrition Facts

Per cookie

Calories	134
Fat	2.8 g
Saturated	1.4 g
Monounsaturated	0.8 g
Polyunsaturated	0.4 g
Carbohydrates	25.8 g
Cholesterol	14.2 mg
Protein	2.4 g
Fiber	1.9 g
Calories from fat	18%

Banana Oatmeal Raisin Cookies

If you have young children around, you should have these cookies around too. It's a great way to use up overripe bananas, and they're fantastic made with chocolate chips instead of raisins.

Preheat the oven to 350°F.

In a medium bowl, beat the butter, sugar and brown sugar until well combined. The mixture will have the consistency of wet sand. Add the bananas, egg and vanilla and beat until well blended, but don't worry about getting out all the banana lumps.

In a medium bowl, stir together the oats, flour, baking soda, cinnamon and salt. Add to the banana mixture and stir by hand until almost combined; add the raisins and stir just until blended.

Drop generous spoonfuls of dough about 2 inches apart on a cookie sheet that has been sprayed with non-stick spray. Bake for 12–14 minutes, until the edges are golden but the cookies are still soft in the middle. Transfer to a wire rack to cool.

Makes 2 dozen cookies.

Inside-Out Chocolate Chunk Cookies

If you prefer, these can be made with regular semi-sweet or mint chocolate chips or chunks, but they look great with white chocolate. They're particularly fantastic eaten warm from the oven, while the chocolate is still soft and gooey.

Preheat the oven to 350°F.

In a large bowl, beat the butter and brown sugar until well combined. The mixture will have the consistency of wet sand. Beat in the egg, egg white, corn syrup and vanilla until smooth.

In a medium bowl, combine the flour, cocoa, baking soda and salt. Add to the sugar mixture and stir by hand until almost combined; add the white chocolate and stir just until blended.

Drop spoonfuls of dough about 2 inches apart on a cookie sheet that has been sprayed with non-stick spray. Bake for 12–14 minutes, until just set around the edges but still soft in the middle. Don't overbake if you want them to be chewy. Transfer to a wire rack to cool.

Makes 1½ dozen cookies.

Chocolate Caramel Chunk Cookies

Chop 20 unwrapped square caramels into quarters with oiled scissors or a knife, and stir into the dough along with the chocolate. Adds just over half a gram of fat per cookie.

Ingredients

¼ cup butter or non-hydrogenated margarine, softened
1 cup packed brown sugar
1 large egg
1 large egg white
3 Tbsp corn syrup
2 tsp vanilla
1½ cups all-purpose flour
¼ cup cocoa
1 tsp baking soda
¼ tsp salt
1 cup white chocolate chunks or chips

Nutrition Facts
Per cookie

Calories	175
Fat	5.9 g
Saturated	3.4 g
Monounsaturated	1.8 g
Polyunsaturated	0.3 g
Carbohydrates	29 g
Cholesterol	21 mg
Protein	2.5 g
Fiber	0.9 g
Calories from fat	30%

Ingredients

¼ cup butter or non-hydrogenated margarine, softened
½ cup sugar
½ cup packed brown sugar
1 large egg or 2 large egg
  whites
2 tsp vanilla
1½ cups all-purpose flour
½ cup cocoa
1 tsp baking soda
¼ tsp salt
⅓ cup strong coffee, cooled
½ cup chocolate chips or
  chunks
½ cup white chocolate chips
  or chunks

Nutrition Facts
Per cookie

Calories	155
Fat	3.9 g
Saturated	2.2 g
Monounsaturated	1.1 g
Polyunsaturated	0.3 g
Carbohydrates	28.3 g
Cholesterol	14 mg
Protein	2.6 g
Fiber	2 g
Calories from fat	22%

Triple Chocolate Chunk Cookies

This is as much chocolate as I could cram into one cookie. If you don't have any white chocolate around, use semi-sweet chocolate chips, or a combination of chopped dark and milk chocolate. When it comes to chocolate, the darker the better: the darker the chocolate, the more antioxidants it contains.

Preheat the oven to 350°F.

In a large bowl, beat the butter, sugar and brown sugar until well blended. It will have the consistency of wet sand. Beat in the egg and vanilla until smooth.

In a medium bowl, stir together the flour, cocoa, baking soda and salt. Add the flour mixture and the coffee to the sugar mixture and stir by hand until almost combined; add the chocolate and stir just until blended.

Drop spoonfuls of dough about 2 inches apart on a cookie sheet that has been sprayed with non-stick spray. Bake for 12–15 minutes, until just set around the edges but still soft in the middle. Don't overbake if you want them to be chewy. Transfer to a wire rack to cool.

Makes 1½ dozen cookies.

Chocolate-Covered Raisin Cookies
Replace the chocolate chips and white chocolate with 1½ cups chocolate covered raisins. Fat is reduced by 1 g per cookie, and you'll benefit from the iron and vitamin B6 in the raisins.

Double Chocolate Apricot Cookies

These are just as the name suggests — chocolate cookies with chocolate chunks and bits of chewy-sweet dried apricots; if you're a fan of apricots and chocolate, you'll like them. Simmering the apricots in orange juice first plumps them up to ensure they don't draw moisture from the batter, which can dry out your cookies no matter what type of dried fruit you're baking with.

Preheat the oven to 350°F.

Place the apricots and orange juice in a small saucepan and bring to a boil over medium heat, or pop them in the microwave for a minute. Remove from the heat and set aside to cool slightly.

In a large bowl, beat the butter, sugar and brown sugar until well blended. Beat in the egg and vanilla until smooth. In a medium bowl, stir together the flour, cocoa, baking soda, baking powder and salt. Add the apricot mixture and the flour mixture to the sugar mixture and stir by hand until almost combined; add the white chocolate and stir just until blended.

Drop round spoonfuls of dough about 2 inches apart on a cookie sheet that has been sprayed with non-stick spray. Bake for 12–15 minutes, until set around the edges but still soft in the middle. Transfer to a wire rack to cool.

Makes 1½ dozen cookies.

Chocolate Apricot & Almond Cookies
Add ½ cup sliced or slivered almonds along with the white chocolate. Adds 2 g fat per cookie, but only the healthy kind.

Ingredients

½ cup chopped dried apricots
½ cup orange juice
¼ cup butter or non-hydrogenated margarine, softened
½ cup sugar
½ cup packed brown sugar
1 large egg or 2 large egg whites
2 tsp vanilla
1½ cups all-purpose flour
½ cup cocoa
½ tsp baking soda
¼ tsp baking powder
¼ tsp salt
½ cup white chocolate chips or chunks

Nutrition Facts
Per cookie

Calories	151
Fat	4.6 g
Saturated	2.6 g
Monounsaturated	1.4 g
Polyunsaturated	0.2 g
Carbohydrates	26.8 g
Cholesterol	20 mg
Protein	2.4 g
Fiber	1.7 g
Calories from fat	26%

Monster Cookies

Monster cookies are traditionally peanut butter-based oatmeal cookies made without flour and studded with some form of chocolate—perfect for the gluten intolerant, or those who run with the gluten intolerant. They're bigger and crispier and keep longer than other drop cookies.

Preheat the oven to 350°F.

Combine the butter and peanut butter in a large bowl. Add the brown sugar, egg, egg white, baking soda and vanilla and beat until smooth. Add the oats, salt, chocolate chips and flaxseed and mix well.

Drop large spoonfuls of dough about 2 inches apart on an ungreased cookie sheet (they'll spread more than regular drop cookies do). Bake for 10–12 minutes, until golden around the edges but still pale in the middle if you want them soft, or golden all over if you want them crunchy. Let them cool for a few minutes on the sheet before transferring to a wire rack.

Makes 2 dozen big cookies.

Ingredients

¼ cup butter or non-hydrogenated margarine, softened
½ cup light or all-natural
  peanut butter
1 cup packed brown sugar
1 large egg
1 large egg white
1 tsp baking soda
2 tsp vanilla
3 cups quick-cooking or old-
  fashioned oats
¼ tsp salt
½ cup chocolate chips or
  M&Ms Minis
¼ cup ground flaxseed
  (optional)

Nutrition Facts
Per cookie

Calories	156
Fat	6.2 g
Saturated	2.6 g
Monounsaturated	2 g
Polyunsaturated	1.2 g
Carbohydrates	22.4 g
Cholesterol	14.5 mg
Protein	3.5 g
Fiber	1.6 g
Calories from fat	35%

Chocolate Oatmeal Cranberry Cookies

OK, these cookies taste better than they look, but I prefer congeniality over beauty any day. Who doesn't love the combination of chocolate and oatmeal? Because these have some texture to them, they're easy to sneak a spoonful of ground flaxseed into.

Preheat the oven to 350°F.

In a large bowl, beat the butter and brown sugar until well blended. It will have the consistency of wet sand. Add the egg, corn syrup and vanilla and beat until smooth.

In a medium bowl, stir together the flour, cocoa, oats, baking soda and salt. Add to the sugar mixture and stir by hand until almost combined; add the cranberries and stir just until blended.

Drop fairly large spoonfuls of dough 2 inches apart on a cookie sheet that has been sprayed with non-stick spray. Bake for 10–12 minutes, until set around the edges but still soft in the middle. They will seem a little undercooked but will firm up as they cool. Transfer to a wire rack to cool.

Makes 20 cookies.

Ingredients

¼ cup butter or non-hydrogenated margarine, softened
1 cup packed brown sugar
1 large egg or 2 large egg whites
2 Tbsp corn syrup
2 tsp vanilla
¾ cup all-purpose flour
¼ cup cocoa
1½ cups oats
½ tsp baking soda
¼ tsp salt
½ cup dried cranberries, cherries or chopped dried apricots

Nutrition Facts
Per cookie

Calories	124
Fat	3.2 g
Saturated	1.6 g
Monounsaturated	1 g
Polyunsaturated	0.3 g
Carbohydrates	22.6 g
Cholesterol	17 mg
Protein	2.1 g
Fiber	1.7 g
Calories from fat	23%

Breakfast Bean Cookies

Packed with protein, fiber, vitamins and minerals, beans are a great way to sneak nutrition into cookies. Puréed, you don't even know they're there! These are substantial, not too sweet, have an amazingly tender texture, and keep longer than other low-fat cookies. I call them breakfast cookies because they make a perfect mobile mini-meal.

Preheat the oven to 350°F.

Place the oats in the bowl of a food processor and pulse until it resembles coarse flour. Add the flour, baking powder, baking soda, cinnamon and salt and process until combined. Transfer to a large bowl.

Put the beans into the food processor and pulse until roughly puréed. Add the butter and process until well blended. Add the brown sugar, egg and vanilla and pulse until smooth, scraping down the sides of the bowl.

Pour the bean mixture into the oat mixture and stir by hand until almost combined; add the chocolate chips, raisins, nuts and flaxseed and stir just until blended.

Drop large spoonfuls of dough onto a cookie sheet that has been sprayed with non-stick spray, and flatten each one a little with your hand. (I find this works best if I dampen my hands first.) Bake for 14–16 minutes, until pale golden around the edges but still soft in the middle. Transfer to a wire rack to cool.

Makes 2 dozen cookies.

Chocolate Lentil Cookies

Use a can of lentils (preferably brown) instead of the white beans, and add ½ cup cocoa to the flour mixture—this helps to disguise the darker color of the lentils. I like to use dried cranberries and apricots instead of raisins when I make this version.

Ingredients

2 cups oats
1 cup all-purpose flour
1 tsp baking powder
1 tsp baking soda
¼ tsp cinnamon (optional)
¼ tsp salt
one 19-oz (540-mL) can white kidney or navy beans, rinsed and drained
¼ cup butter or non-hydrogenated margarine, softened
1 cup packed brown sugar
1 large egg
2 tsp vanilla
½ cup chocolate chips
½ cup raisins or dried cranberries
¼–½ cup chopped walnuts
2–4 Tbsp ground flaxseed

Nutrition Facts

Per cookie

Calories	165
Fat	4.9 g
Saturated	2.3 g
Monounsaturated	1.3 g
Polyunsaturated	1 g
Carbohydrates	27.3 g
Cholesterol	14.5 mg
Protein	3.4 g
Fiber	2.4 g
Calories from fat	26%

Almond Butter Chocolate Chip Cookies

Although these are distractingly good, to the point where I can hardly stand keeping them in the same vicinity as me, the almond flavor isn't as pronounced as you might expect it to be considering the amount of almond butter in them. If you want a more almondy flavor, use almond extract instead of (or as well as) the vanilla. Almond butter is becoming almost as popular as peanut butter on store shelves, and almonds are very high in calcium as well as fiber, protein, vitamins and other minerals. Other nut butters make delicious cookies too—try hazelnut, cashew or pecan.

Preheat the oven to 350°F.

In a large bowl, beat the almond butter, margarine, sugar and brown sugar with an electric mixer until well combined. Add the egg and vanilla and beat again.

Add the flour, baking soda and salt and beat on low speed or stir by hand to incorporate it into the dough. It will be dry and crumbly, and you may need to use your hands. About halfway through the mixing, add the chocolate chips and stir just until blended.

Almond butters tend to vary, so the way your dough ends up depends on what type you used, but it will probably be oily and crumbly. Shape the dough into balls a bit bigger than a walnut, and place at least an inch apart on an ungreased cookie sheet. If you'd like to help get them started spreading, flatten each one a little with the palm of your hand, so they're more like little patties.

Bake for about 12 minutes, until just set.

Makes 2 dozen cookies.

Ingredients

1 cup almond butter (stir it first, as it tends to separate in the jar)
¼ cup non-hydrogenated margarine or butter, softened
½ cup sugar
½ cup packed brown sugar
1 large egg
2 tsp vanilla
1½ cups all-purpose flour
1 tsp baking soda
¼ tsp salt
1 cup chocolate chips or chopped semi-sweet or dark chocolate

Nutrition Facts
Per cookie

Calories	202
Fat	11 g
Saturated	3.5 g
Monounsaturated	5.3 g
Polyunsaturated	1.8 g
Carbohydrates	23.5 g
Cholesterol	14.8 mg
Protein	3.3 g
Fiber	1.3 g
Calories from fat	48%

Black & White Cookies

The Black & White cookie is native to New York, and was made famous by the Seinfeld episode in which Jerry breaks the no-vomit streak he had held since June 29, 1980. Black & white cookies are larger and more cake-like than most, and most have a slight lemon flavor, sometimes in the cookie itself but more often in the icing. I tested these with a friend addicted to cookies straight from New York, and she says these are even better.

Preheat oven to 350°F.

In a large bowl, beat together the butter and sugar for a minute, until pale and fluffy. Add the egg and beat until smooth.

In a small bowl, stir together the flour, baking soda and salt. Add about a third of it to the butter mixture and stir by hand just until combined. Add half the buttermilk and stir again, then another third of the flour, the rest of the buttermilk, and the rest of the flour, stirring just until combined.

Drop ¼ cup of batter about 2 inches apart on a cookie sheet that has been sprayed with non-stick spray. Bake for 15–20 minutes, until golden around the edges and the middles are springy to the touch. Transfer to a wire rack to cool.

To make the icings, stir together the icing sugar, corn syrup, lemon juice and 1 Tbsp water until smooth, adding a little extra sugar or water if you need it to make a spreadable icing with a slightly fluid consistency. Transfer half the icing to a separate bowl and stir in the cocoa and remaining 1 Tbsp water and stir until it has the same consistency.

Frost the completely cooled cookies with half chocolate, half white icing. Traditionally this is done on the bottom (flat side) of the cookie, but you can frost whichever side you like.

Makes 10 cookies.

Ingredients

Cookies
¼ cup butter or non-hydrogenated margarine, softened
½ cup sugar
1 large egg
1¼ cups all-purpose flour
½ tsp baking soda
¼ tsp salt
⅓ cup buttermilk

Icings
1½ cups icing sugar
1 Tbsp corn syrup or honey
2 tsp lemon juice or water
1–2 Tbsp. water
¼ cup cocoa

Nutrition Facts

Per cookie

Calories	227
Fat	5.5 g
Saturated	3.2 g
Monounsaturated	1.6 g
Polyunsaturated	0.3 g
Carbohydrates	43 g
Cholesterol	34 mg
Protein	3 g
Fiber	1.5 g
Calories from fat	21%

Crispy Chocolate Walnut Cookies

Those who appreciate crispy cookies will love these. Walnuts contain more protein than almonds or pecans, and are high in antioxidants and ALA, a plant-based omega-3 fatty acid. Many people think they don't like walnuts because of their bitter taste; this is usually because the nuts are rancid. Ensure you always have a fresh stash of walnuts, and store them in the fridge or freezer to keep them that way.

In a medium bowl, beat the egg and egg white with an electric mixer for a minute, until thick and pale. Sprinkle flour, baking powder and salt over the eggs, and gently stir to combine.

Fold the melted chocolate into the egg mixture along with the vanilla and nuts. Cover and chill the dough for an hour, or overnight.

When ready to bake, preheat the oven to 375°F. Drop spoonfuls of dough 2–3 inches apart on a cookie sheet that has been sprayed with non-stick spray. Bake for 12–15 minutes. Let cool for a few minutes on the cookie sheet before transferring to a wire rack to cool.

Makes 1½ dozen cookies.

Ingredients

1 large egg
1 large egg white
1 cup sugar
⅔ cup all-purpose flour
1 tsp baking powder
¼ tsp salt
2 oz semi-sweet chocolate,
  melted (2 squares)
1 tsp vanilla
⅔ cup finely chopped walnuts
  or pecans

Nutrition Facts
Per cookie

Calories	110
Fat	4.1 g
Saturated	0.9 g
Monounsaturated	1.1 g
Polyunsaturated	1.8 g
Carbohydrates	17 g
Cholesterol	12 mg
Protein	2.3 g
Fiber	0.6 g
Calories from fat	32%

Macaroons

More than half the coconut has been replaced by corn flakes, making traditional macaroons much lower in fat and calories.

Preheat the oven to 350°F.

In a medium bowl, beat the egg whites, vanilla and salt until foamy. Gradually add sugar, beating until stiff and glossy. Fold in the coconut and corn flakes.

Drop spoonfuls of the mixture onto a cookie sheet that has been lined with foil and sprayed with non-stick spray. Bake for 10–12 minutes, until very pale golden.

Makes 1 dozen macaroons.

Ingredients

2 large egg whites
½ tsp coconut or vanilla extract
pinch salt
½ cup sugar
½ cup shredded coconut
1 cup corn flakes

Nutrition Facts

Per cookie

Calories	79
Fat	1 g
Saturated	0.9 g
Monounsaturated	0 g
Polyunsaturated	0 g
Carbohydrates	16.6 g
Cholesterol	0 mg
Protein	1 g
Fiber	0.4 g
Calories from fat	11%

Chocolate Pecan Brown Sugar Bundles

The one downfall of low-fat cookies is their inability to stay fresh for days at a time; this isn't a problem with these meringue-wrapped bundles of chocolate and nuts, which are crunchy on the outside, marshmallowy on the inside. They're also great with the addition of chopped dried apricots.

Preheat the oven to 300°F. Line two cookie sheets with aluminum foil. (Lightly dampening the sheet first will help the foil stay in place.) Spray the foil with non-stick spray.

In a clean, dry glass or stainless steel bowl, beat the egg whites, cream of tartar and salt until soft peaks form. Gradually add the brown sugar and beat until the mixture is glossy and stiff.

Sprinkle flour, chocolate chips and pecans over the top and gently fold in, mixing just until combined.

Drop large, rounded spoonfuls of batter about 2 inches apart on one of the prepared cookie sheets. Bake for 20 minutes, then turn the oven off and let the cookies sit in the warm oven for another 20 minutes.

Slide the entire sheet of foil off the cookie sheet and place on a wire rack to cool. Reheat the oven and repeat with the remaining batter. When completely cool, gently peel the cookies off the foil. Store extras in a tightly sealed container.

Makes 1½ dozen bundles.

Ingredients

3 large egg whites
¼ tsp cream of tartar
¼ tsp salt
1 cup packed brown sugar
3 Tbsp all-purpose flour
½ cup chocolate chips, chopped, or mini chocolate chips
½ cup chopped pecans

Nutrition Facts
Per bundle

Calories	109
Fat	3.8 g
Saturated	1.3 g
Monounsaturated	1.7 g
Polyunsaturated	0.7 g
Carbohydrates	18 g
Cholesterol	0.4 mg
Protein	1.4 g
Fiber	0.7 g
Calories from fat	30%

Ingredients

1⅓ cups semi-sweet chocolate chips (divided)
1 square unsweetened chocolate (1 oz)
1 Tbsp butter or non-hydrogenated margarine
⅔ cup sugar
½ cup all-purpose flour
1 Tbsp cocoa
¼ tsp baking soda
¼ tsp salt
1 large egg
1 large egg white
1 tsp vanilla

Nutrition Facts

Per cookie

Calories	156
Fat	6.6 g
Saturated	4 g
Monounsaturated	1.8 g
Polyunsaturated	0.7 g
Carbohydrates	22.6 g
Cholesterol	15 mg
Protein	2.3 g
Fiber	1.7 g
Calories from fat	37%

Chocolate Bliss

These are like rich, dark and intense chocolate brownies in cookie form. Though a little higher in fat than most in this book, they still have less than half the fat of a typical small unfrosted brownie.

Combine 1 cup of the chocolate chips, the unsweetened chocolate and butter in a double boiler (just a stainless steel or glass bowl) set over hot water. Stir until melted and smooth. Remove from the heat and scrape into a large bowl. (Alternately, melt these ingredients in a glass bowl in the microwave.)

In a medium bowl, stir together the sugar, flour, cocoa, baking soda and salt. Add to the chocolate mixture along with the egg, egg white and vanilla. Stir by hand until almost combined; add the remaining ⅓ cup chocolate chips and stir just until blended.

If it's too sticky to handle, cover and chill the dough in the refrigerator for about ½ hour, until it firms up a little. Preheat the oven to 350°F.

Drop spoonfuls of dough 2 inches apart on a cookie sheet that has been sprayed with non-stick spray. Bake for 12–15 minutes, until the edges are set but the cookies are still soft in the middle. Transfer to a wire rack to cool.

Makes 1½ dozen cookies.

Chocolate Peanut Butter Oat Cookies

In a prime example of necessity being the mother of invention, I came up with these to bring to a TV crew one day, when one person couldn't eat flour or dairy. I substituted peanut butter for half the butter; non-hydrogenated margarine for the rest, and used a combination of oat flour and oats for the flour. The result—cookies that no one could tell were flour-free and everyone went crazy for! The nutty flavor of the oats makes the best possible chocolate chip cookies, especially with the combination of peanuts and peanut butter.

Preheat the oven to 350°F.

In a large bowl, beat the margarine or butter, peanut butter and brown sugar until well combined. Add the egg and vanilla and beat until smooth.

Add the oat flour, oats, baking soda and salt to the butter-sugar mixture and stir by hand until almost combined; add the chocolate chips, peanuts, sunflower seeds and cranberries and stir just until blended.

Roll dough into 1½-inch balls and place them about 2 inches apart on a cookie sheet that has been sprayed with non-stick spray. Bake for 12–15 minutes, or until pale golden and just set around the edges but still soft in the middle. Don't overbake if you want them to be chewy. Transfer to a wire rack to cool.

Makes 1½ dozen cookies.

Ingredients

¼ cup non-hydrogenated margarine or butter, softened
¼ cup all-natural peanut butter
1 cup packed brown sugar
1 large egg
2 tsp vanilla
1 cup oat flour
1½ cups oats
½ tsp baking soda
¼ tsp salt
½ cup chocolate chips
½ cup salted peanuts, walnuts or pecans
¼ cup sunflower seeds (optional)
¼ cup dried cranberries (optional)

Nutrition Facts
Per cookie

Calories	155
Fat	5 g
Saturated	3 g
Monounsaturated	1.4 g
Polyunsaturated	0.5 g
Carbohydrates	25.5 g
Cholesterol	17.6 mg
Protein	2 g
Fiber	1 g
Calories from fat	29%

Carrot Cake Cookies

Carrot seems to be one of the most popular cake flavors, so why not a cookie version? These have a texture similar to carrot cake, and work well with whole wheat flour, or half all-purpose and half whole wheat. For a true carrot cake experience, slather the bottoms of cooled cookies with cream cheese frosting and sandwich with another cookie.

Preheat the oven to 350°F.

In a large bowl, beat the butter, sugar, brown sugar, egg and vanilla until well blended and smooth. Add the flour, cinnamon, baking soda, salt and carrots and stir by hand until almost blended; add the raisins and nuts and stir just until combined.

Drop spoonfuls of dough onto a cookie sheet that has been sprayed with non-stick spray. Bake for 12–14 minutes, until they're just barely golden around the edges and on the lumpy parts, but still soft in the middle and not wet-looking on top. Transfer to a wire rack to cool.

Once the cookies have completely cooled, you can frost them with cream cheese frosting, or make sandwiches by frosting the bottom of a cookie and sandwiching it with another.

Makes 1½ dozen cookies.

Ingredients

¼ cup butter or non-hydrogenated margarine, softened
½ cup sugar
½ cup packed brown sugar
1 large egg
1 tsp vanilla
1½ cups all-purpose flour
1 tsp cinnamon
½ tsp baking soda
¼ tsp salt
1 packed cup coarsely grated carrot (about 2 carrots)
½ cup raisins or dried cranberries
¼ cup chopped walnuts or pecans (optional)
Lemon Cream Cheese Frosting (optional, see page 198)

Nutrition Facts

Per cookie

Calories	128
Fat	3 g
Saturated	1.7 g
Monounsaturated	0.9 g
Polyunsaturated	0.2 g
Carbohydrates	24.2 g
Cholesterol	19 mg
Protein	1.7 g
Fiber	1 g
Calories from fat	21%

Pumpkin Hermits

The term "hermit" refers to soft molasses and spice cookies made with raisins and nuts, and to be honest I have no idea why. Adding pumpkin boosts the nutritional value of these cookies, but don't think you have to buy fresh pumpkin and clean out all the squidgy goo; cup for cup, canned pumpkin has about 20 times the beta carotene of fresh, making these an excellent source of beta carotene and magnesium.

Preheat the oven to 350°F.

In a medium bowl, stir together the flour, cinnamon, allspice, ginger, baking powder, baking soda and salt; set aside.

In a large bowl, beat the butter, brown sugar, pumpkin, egg, molasses and vanilla until smooth. Add the flour mixture and stir by hand until almost combined; add the raisins or other dried fruit and stir just until blended.

Drop large, rounded spoonfuls of dough 2 inches apart on a cookie sheet that has been sprayed with non-stick spray. Bake for 12–14 minutes, until just set — springy to the touch around the edges, but you still leave a slight dent if you touch them in the middle. Transfer to a wire rack to cool.

Makes 2 dozen cookies.

Ingredients

2 cups all-purpose flour
1 tsp cinnamon
½ tsp ground allspice
½ tsp ground ginger
1 tsp baking powder
½ tsp baking soda
¼ tsp salt
¼ cup butter or non-hydrogenated margarine, melted
1 cup packed brown sugar
¾ cup canned pure pumpkin
1 large egg
¼ cup dark molasses
1 tsp vanilla
1½ cups raisins, dried cranberries and/or chopped dried apricots

Nutrition Facts

Per cookie

Calories	136
Fat	2.3 g
Saturated	1.3 g
Monounsaturated	0.6 g
Polyunsaturated	0.2 g
Carbohydrates	28.2 g
Cholesterol	14.2 mg
Protein	1.8 g
Fiber	1.2 g
Calories from fat	15%

Ingredients

1 medium-large tart apple
(such as Granny Smith
or McIntosh)
1 cup all-purpose flour
¾ cup whole wheat flour
1 cup packed brown sugar
½ tsp baking soda
½ tsp cinnamon
¼ tsp salt
1 cup grated old cheddar
cheese
¼ cup canola oil, flax oil or
butter or non-hydrogenated
margarine, melted
¼ cup milk
1 large egg
2 tsp vanilla
½ cup raisins or dried cranberries, or a combination
¼ cup chopped walnuts or
pecans

Nutrition Facts

Per cookie

Calories	162
Fat	5.5 g
Saturated	1 g
Monounsaturated	2.4 g
Polyunsaturated	1.7 g
Carbohydrates	26.2 g
Cholesterol	15 mg
Protein	3.1 g
Fiber	1.4 g
Calories from fat	30%

Fresh Apple & Cheddar Hermits

Researchers at Yale discovered that the fragrance of apples, baked apples and mulled cider had a calming effect and actually reduced anxiety attacks. See? Cookies really can reduce stress. You need to use old cheddar in these so that the cheesy flavor comes through.

Preheat the oven to 350°F. Core and finely chop or grate the apple—you can peel it first, but I like to leave the skin on.

In a large bowl, stir together the flours, brown sugar, baking soda, cinnamon and salt. Add the grated cheddar and toss to combine.

In a small bowl, whisk together the oil, milk, egg and vanilla. Add to the flour mixture and stir by hand until almost combined. Add the apples, raisins and walnuts and stir just until blended.

Drop large spoonfuls of dough about 2 inches apart on a cookie sheet that has been sprayed with non-stick spray. Bake for 12–15 minutes, until golden around the edges and just set in the middle. Transfer to a wire rack to cool.

Because of the moistness of these cookies, they shouldn't be stored in an airtight container or they tend to become gummy. Store in a loosely covered container or on a plate covered with a tea towel.

Makes 1½ dozen cookies.

Grandma Woodall's Marmalade Cookies

Baking was just one of my Grandma's many talents, and these oatmeal-raisin cookies were one of her specialties. They're big and crispy, mildly spiced and the marmalade adds a wonderful flavor along with bits of orange and citrus. Grandma preferred Robertson's Thick Cut Marmalade. She said, "It gives them that extra zip!" Adjust the spices if you like, using more or less of each to suit your taste. If you choose to use fresh grated ginger (I do), add it to the butter-sugar mixture.

Preheat the oven to 350°F.

In a medium bowl, combine the flour, oats, baking powder, baking soda, salt, cinnamon, ginger and nutmeg; set aside.

In a large bowl, beat together the butter, sugar and brown sugar until well combined. It will have the consistency of wet sand. Beat in the egg and vanilla until smooth.

Add the flour mixture to the butter mixture and stir by hand until almost combined; add the raisins and marmalade, and stir just until blended.

Drop fairly large spoonfuls of dough a good 2 inches apart (they spread larger and flatter than normal drop cookies do) on a cookie sheet that has been sprayed with non-stick spray. Bake for 15–20 minutes, until deep golden all over. Cool for a few minutes on the cookie sheet, then transfer to a wire rack to cool completely.

Makes 2 dozen cookies.

Ingredients

1 cup all-purpose flour
1¼ cups oats
½ tsp baking powder
½ tsp baking soda
½ tsp salt
½ tsp cinnamon
½ tsp ground ginger (or 1 tsp grated fresh)
¼ tsp nutmeg
¼ cup butter or non-hydrogenated margarine, softened
½ cup sugar
½ cup packed brown sugar
1 large egg
1 tsp vanilla
1 cup raisins
⅓ cup marmalade

Nutrition Facts
Per cookie

Calories	125
Fat	2.6 g
Saturated	1.3 g
Monounsaturated	0.7 g
Polyunsaturated	0.3 g
Carbohydrates	24.6 g
Cholesterol	14.2 mg
Protein	1.8 g
Fiber	1.2 g
Calories from fat	18%

Molasses Crinkles

Cinnamon Sugar Phyllo Twists

Whole Wheat Snickerdoodles

Peanut Butter Cookies

Chunky Peanut Crunch Cookies

Chocolate Thumbprints

Chocolava

Cornmeal Maple Pecan Twists

Devil's Food Crackles

Russian Tea Cakes

Green Tea Cookies

Fortune Cookies

Almond Macaroons

Multigrain Shortbread

Old-Fashioned Sour Cream Sugar Cookies

Chocolate, Pecan & Olive Oil Wafers

Espresso Bean Cookies

Corn Flake Cookies

Whoopie Pies

Shaped Cookies

Molasses Crinkles

It's funny how when you ask someone what their favorite cookie is, the answer is generally chocolate chip or peanut butter, yet every time I pull out a batch of these everyone tells me it's their favorite kind. Make sure you don't overbake them; they need to stay chewy.

Preheat the oven to 350°F.

In a large bowl, combine the oil, butter, molasses, brown sugar, egg whites and vanilla. Stir until well blended and smooth.

In a medium bowl, stir together the flour, baking soda, cinnamon, ginger, allspice and salt; add to the molasses mixture and stir by hand just until you have a soft dough.

Roll dough into 1–1½-inch balls and roll the balls in sugar to coat. Place them about 2 inches apart on a cookie sheet that has been sprayed with non-stick spray.

Bake for 12–14 minutes, until just set around the edges. Transfer to a wire rack to cool or serve warm. Store extras in an airtight container or freeze.

Makes 20 cookies.

Lemon-Ginger Ice Cream Sandwiches

Stir ¼ cup thawed lemonade concentrate into 1 L softened light vanilla ice cream; place a scoop onto one cookie and top with another. Press down gently until the ice cream spreads to the edges. (This is easier if the cookies are frozen first.) Wrap individually in plastic wrap and freeze until firm.

Ingredients

2 Tbsp butter or non-hydrogenated margarine, softened
2 Tbsp canola or flax oil
⅓ cup dark molasses
1 cup packed brown sugar
1 large egg
2 tsp vanilla
2 cups all-purpose flour
2 tsp baking soda
1 Tbsp cinnamon
1½ tsp ground ginger
½ tsp ground allspice
¼ tsp salt
extra sugar, for rolling

Nutrition Facts
Per cookie

Calories	134
Fat	2.9 g
Saturated	0.9 g
Monounsaturated	1.2 g
Polyunsaturated	0.5 g
Carbohydrates	25.5 g
Cholesterol	14 mg
Protein	1.6 g
Fiber	0.5 g
Calories from fat	19%

Cinnamon Sugar Phyllo Twists

If you've ever worked with phyllo pastry, chances are you've been left with a few sheets from a package. This is a great way to use them up. Each sheet of phyllo dough contains only half a gram of fat; the pastry only becomes unhealthy when the layers are brushed with copious amounts of melted butter. Some low-fat cookbooks suggest spraying your layers with non-stick spray instead, but would you spray your bread with non-stick spray? If you brush sparingly and sprinkle with a little sugar, you'll end up with light and buttery pastry with a fraction of the fat of traditional rolled pastry. It's the perfect example of how a little butter can go a long way.

Preheat the oven to 350°F.

Combine the sugar and cinnamon in a small dish.

Lay 1 sheet of phyllo on a clean, dry surface, keeping the remainder covered with a tea towel. Brush lightly with some of the butter, and sprinkle with cinnamon sugar, using about 1/5 of each. Repeat with the next 4 sheets, then top with the last sheet of phyllo. Press down gently to help the layers stick to each other.

Cut the stack of phyllo lengthwise, then widthwise in half, to make quarters. Working with one quarter at a time (keep the others covered), cut lengthwise into 4 strips, then in half widthwise to make eight 1½- × 4-inch strips. Twist each strip once to make a little bowtie, and place ½–1-inch apart on a cookie sheet lightly sprayed with non-stick spray.

Bake for 10–12 minutes, until golden. Transfer to a wire rack to cool. Sprinkle cooled cookies with icing sugar.

Makes about 3 dozen twists.

Ingredients

6 sheets phyllo dough, thawed
⅓ cup sugar
½ tsp cinnamon
2 Tbsp butter, melted
icing sugar for sprinkling
   (optional)

Nutrition Facts
Per twist

Calories	22
Fat	0.8 g
Saturated	0.4 g
Monounsaturated	0.2 g
Polyunsaturated	0.1 g
Carbohydrates	3.5 g
Cholesterol	1.7 mg
Protein	0.2 g
Fiber	0 g
Calories from fat	33%

Ingredients

¼ cup butter or non-hydrogenated margarine, softened
1 cup packed brown sugar
1 large egg
1 Tbsp corn syrup
2 tsp vanilla
1 cup flour
½ cup whole wheat flour
1 tsp baking soda
1 tsp cinnamon
¼ tsp salt
sugar, for rolling
cinnamon, for rolling

Nutrition Facts
Per cookie

Calories	119
Fat	3 g
Saturated	1.7 g
Monounsaturated	0.9 g
Polyunsaturated	0.2 g
Carbohydrates	22 g
Cholesterol	19 mg
Protein	1.6 g
Fiber	0.7 g
Calories from fat	22%

Whole Wheat Snickerdoodles

Using whole wheat flour adds a nutty flavor as well as fiber to these mildly spiced cookies. If you like, they can be made using only all-purpose flour, or experiment with different flours such as rye, spelt or kamut.

Preheat the oven to 350°F.

In a large bowl, beat the butter and brown sugar until well combined. The mixture will have the consistency of wet sand. Beat in the egg, corn syrup and vanilla until smooth.

In a medium bowl, stir together the flour, whole wheat flour, baking soda, cinnamon and salt. Add to the sugar mixture and stir by hand just until combined.

In a shallow dish, stir together about ½ cup sugar and 2 tsp cinnamon. Roll the dough into walnut-sized balls and roll in cinnamon sugar to coat. Place about 2 inches apart on a cookie sheet sprayed with non-stick spray.

Bake for 12–15 minutes, or until pale golden around the edges but still soft in the middle. Transfer to a wire rack to cool.

Makes 1½ dozen cookies.

LEFT TO RIGHT: Whole Wheat Snickerdoodles p. 60; Chocolate Cream Cheese Sandwich Cookies p. 87; Chocolate Bliss p. 50; Butter Pecan Diamonds p. 86

Peanut Butter Cookies

I should have named these "the best ever" or some such, because this is the recipe people most often rave about. There's no typo — it really doesn't contain any flour. This means there's nothing to dilute their peanut buttery flavor. You can use all white sugar or all brown, but I usually use half of each. The dough may seem too wet at first, but as you stir, it will stiffen up, like a delicious science experiment. Yum.

Preheat the oven to 350°F.

In a medium bowl, mix the peanut butter, sugar, brown sugar and egg white until completely blended.

Roll the dough into 1–1½-inch balls and place about 2 inches apart on an ungreased cookie sheet. Press down on each cookie once or twice (crisscrossed) with the back of a fork.

Bake for 12–15 minutes, until pale golden and set around the edges. Gently transfer to a wire rack to cool. If they're too crumbly to move, let them cool for a minute or two on the cookie sheet first.

Makes 2 dozen cookies.

Peanut Butter White Chocolate Chunk Cookies
Add ½ cup white chocolate chips or chunks to the dough. Adds 1 g fat per cookie.

PB & J Thumbprints
Add 1 cup all-purpose or whole wheat flour to the dough and roll it into walnut-sized balls. Place them on a cookie sheet and make a small indent in each with your thumb; fill each dent with jam. Bake as directed. Fat content remains the same.

Ingredients

1½ cups light, regular or all-
    natural peanut butter
½ cup sugar
½ cup packed brown sugar
1 large egg white

Nutrition Facts

Per cookie

Calories	110
Fat	5.6 g
Saturated	1 g
Monounsaturated	2.4 g
Polyunsaturated	1.9 g
Carbohydrates	13.7 g
Cholesterol	0 mg
Protein	3 g
Fiber	0.8 g
Calories from fat	43%

Chunky Peanut Crunch Cookies

Peanut butter cookies are enormously popular, so I'm always surprised at the lack of variations on the theme. These are chunky with real peanuts, and the bits of chewy, sweet ruby-red cherries make them reminiscent of PB&J.

Preheat the oven to 325°F.

Place the peanuts in a food processor with a few spoonfuls of the sugar. Pulse until the nuts are coarsely chopped.

In a large bowl, stir together the remaining sugar, peanut butter, egg white, milk and vanilla until smooth. Add flour, baking soda, salt and peanuts and stir until almost combined; add the dried cherries and stir just until blended.

Roll the dough into 1-inch balls and place them about an inch apart on a cookie sheet that has been sprayed with non-stick spray. Flatten each cookie a little with a fork or your hand. Bake for 14–16 minutes, until pale golden around the edges. Transfer to a wire rack to cool.

Makes 1½ dozen cookies.

Ingredients

1 cup salted, dry roasted or
   honey roasted peanuts
¾ cup sugar (white or brown)
3 Tbsp light or all-natural
   peanut butter
1 large egg white
2 Tbsp milk
1 tsp vanilla
½ cup all-purpose flour
½ cup whole wheat flour
½ tsp baking soda
pinch salt
⅓ cup dried cherries or
   cranberries, coarsely
   chopped (optional)

Nutrition Facts
Per cookie

Calories	119
Fat	5.1 g
Saturated	0.8 g
Monounsaturated	2.4 g
Polyunsaturated	1.6 g
Carbohydrates	16 g
Cholesterol	0 mg
Protein	3.5 g
Fiber	1.2 g
Calories from fat	37%

Ingredients

¼ cup butter or non-hydroge-
    nated margarine, softened
½ cup sugar
¼ cup packed brown sugar
2 Tbsp corn syrup
1 large egg
1 tsp vanilla
½ tsp instant coffee granules,
    dissolved in 1 tsp water
1½ cups all-purpose flour
⅓ cup cocoa
½ tsp baking powder
¼ tsp baking soda
¼ tsp salt
¼–⅓ cup raspberry, cherry or
    apricot jam
icing sugar, for sprinkling
    (optional)

Nutrition Facts

Per cookie

Calories	90
Fat	2.3 g
Saturated	1.3 g
Monounsaturated	0.7 g
Polyunsaturated	0.1 g
Carbohydrates	16.5 g
Cholesterol	14.2 mg
Protein	1.4 g
Fiber	0.8 g
Calories from fat	22%

Chocolate Thumbprints

Jam-filled thumbprint cookies have that nostalgic charm reserved for dainties served at my grandma's church events and Christmas bazaar. All types of jam go well with chocolate, or replace the cocoa with a little more flour for plain butter cookies.

Preheat the oven to 375°F.

In a large bowl, beat the butter, sugar and brown sugar until well blended. Beat in the corn syrup, egg, vanilla and coffee until smooth.

In a medium bowl, stir together the flour, cocoa, baking powder, baking soda and salt. Add to the butter-sugar mixture and stir by hand just until you have a soft dough.

Roll the dough into 1–1½-inch balls and place them about an inch apart on a cookie sheet sprayed with non-stick spray. Make indentations in the middle of each cookie with your thumb and fill each dent with jam.

Bake the cookies for 12–14 minutes, until just set around the edges. Transfer to a wire rack to cool. If you like, sprinkle cooled cookies with icing sugar before serving.

Makes 2 dozen cookies.

Double Chocolate Kisses

Instead of filling with jam, press an unwrapped chocolate Hershey's Kiss into each ball of dough. Bake as directed. Adds 1.5 g Fat per cookie.

Chocolate Cheesecake Thumbprints

Beat 4 oz light cream cheese and ¼ cup sugar until smooth; beat in an egg white and ¼ tsp vanilla. Refrigerate for about 30 minutes, or up to 24 hours. Fill cookies with a small spoonful of batter and bake as directed. Adds 0.3 g fat per cookie.

Chocolava

This is The One—the cookie that started it all. When I had a bakery, they were my biggest seller, generating requests from across Canada and as far away as San Francisco. Chocolavas are rich chocolate brownie-like cookies rolled in icing sugar before they're baked to create a crackled surface (hence the lava reference) as they rise and spread in the oven.

Preheat the oven to 350°F.

In a large bowl or in the bowl of a food processor, combine the flour, sugar, brown sugar, cocoa, baking powder and salt, breaking up any lumps of brown sugar. Add the butter and pulse or stir with a fork, pastry cutter or whisk until the mixture is well combined and crumbly.

Add the eggs and vanilla and stir by hand just until the dough comes together. The dough will be fairly dry. It will seem at first that there isn't enough moisture, but if you keep stirring, or get in there and use your fingers, it will eventually come together.

Place a few heaping spoonfuls of icing sugar into a shallow dish. Roll the dough into 1½-inch balls and roll the balls in icing sugar to coat. Place them about 2 inches apart on a cookie sheet that has been sprayed with non-stick spray. Bake for 12–14 minutes, until just set around the edges but still soft in the middle. Transfer to a wire rack to cool.

Makes 20 cookies.

Ingredients

1⅓ cups all-purpose flour
1 cup sugar
⅓ cup packed brown sugar
½ cup cocoa
1 tsp baking powder
¼ tsp salt
¼ cup butter or non-hydrogenated margarine, softened
2 large eggs or 3 large egg whites, lightly beaten
2 tsp vanilla
icing sugar, for rolling

Nutrition Facts
Per cookie

Calories	111
Fat	2.6 g
Saturated	1.5 g
Monounsaturated	0.7 g
Polyunsaturated	0.1 g
Carbohydrates	21.3 g
Cholesterol	6.2 mg
Protein	1.8 g
Fiber	1.3 g
Calories from fat	20%

Ingredients

½ cup pecans (pieces or
    halves)
½ cup sugar
1¼ cups all-purpose flour
¼ cup yellow cornmeal
¼ tsp baking powder
¼ tsp salt
¼ cup butter, softened
1 large egg, lightly beaten
3 Tbsp pure maple syrup
icing sugar for dipping

Nutrition Facts

Per cookie

Calories	93
Fat	3.7 g
Saturated	1.4 g
Monounsaturated	1.6 g
Polyunsaturated	0.5 g
Carbohydrates	14 g
Cholesterol	14.2 mg
Protein	1.3 g
Fiber	0.4 g
Calories from fat	35%

Cornmeal Maple Pecan Twists

Common in cornbread, the combination of cornmeal, maple and pecans is very different but utterly delicious in a cookie. If you find the "S" shapes too finicky, shape them into crescents or rings instead.

Preheat the oven to 350°F.

Place the pecans in a food processor with a few spoonfuls of the sugar, and pulse until finely ground. Add the remaining sugar, flour, cornmeal, baking powder and salt and pulse until blended. Add the butter and pulse until you have a coarse meal.

Dump the mixture into a large bowl and add the egg and maple syrup; stir just until the dough comes together. Pinch off 1–1½-inch pieces of dough and roll into 4–5-inch long ropes. Shape each rope into an "S" shape and place about 1 inch apart on a cookie sheet sprayed with non-stick spray.

Bake for 12–14 minutes, until golden on the bottoms. As soon as they come out of the oven, dip the cookies in icing sugar to coat before placing on a wire rack to cool.

Makes 2 dozen cookies.

Devil's Food Crackles

Here's a great way to use up any cake mixes you picked up on sale — they make better cookies than they do cakes!

Preheat the oven to 350°F.

In a large bowl, combine the cake mix, oil and egg whites and stir just until blended. Shape the dough into 1–1½-inch balls, and roll the balls in sugar or icing sugar to coat.

Place them 2 inches apart on a cookie sheet that has been sprayed with non-stick spray. Bake for 12–14 minutes, until just set around the edges but still soft in the middle. Transfer to a wire rack to cool.

Makes 2 dozen cookies.

Ingredients

one 510-g pkg devil's food or
    other chocolate cake mix
¼ cup canola oil, butter or non-
    hydrogenated margarine,
    melted
3 large egg whites or 2 large
    eggs
sugar or icing sugar, for rolling

Nutrition Facts
Per cookie

Calories	112
Fat	4.8 g
Saturated	0.8 g
Monounsaturated	3.3 g
Polyunsaturated	0.9 g
Carbohydrates	17.4 g
Cholesterol	0 mg
Protein	1.5 g
Fiber	0.6 g
Calories from fat	36%

Russian Tea Cakes

Also known as Mexican Wedding Cakes, or in my mom's cookbook, Nut Balls, these buttery shortbread-like morsels usually get their melt-in-your-mouth texture from butter, and lots of it. These contain about half the fat, but the addition of cornstarch means they still melt in your mouth.

Preheat the oven to 350°F.

Place the nuts in a dry baking pan and toast in the oven (you can do it on the stovetop instead if you like) for 5–8 minutes, until lightly browned and fragrant. Give the pan a shake once in a while to ensure even browning. Cool and finely chop by hand or in a food processor.

In a medium bowl, stir together the flour, cornstarch, salt and nuts; set aside. In a large bowl, beat the butter, oil and icing sugar with an electric mixer for 2 minutes, until light and fluffy. Add the milk and vanilla and beat until smooth.

Add the flour mixture to the butter mixture and stir by hand just until the dough comes together. Shape into walnut-sized balls and place about an inch apart on an ungreased cookie sheet.

Bake for 12–15 minutes, until golden on the bottoms. Meanwhile, put some icing sugar in a shallow dish. Remove cookies from the cookie sheet while they're still hot and immediately roll in icing sugar to coat them, then place on a wire rack to cool.

Makes 2 dozen cookies.

Ingredients

¾ cup pecans, hazelnuts, walnuts, almonds or a combination
1½ cups all-purpose flour
¼ cup cornstarch
¼ tsp salt
⅓ cup butter (don't use margarine), softened
1 Tbsp canola oil
¾ cup icing sugar
2 Tbsp milk
1 tsp vanilla
icing sugar, for rolling

Nutrition Facts
Per cookie

Calories	104
Fat	5.5 g
Saturated	1.8 g
Monounsaturated	2.5 g
Polyunsaturated	0.9 g
Carbohydrates	12.9 g
Cholesterol	7 mg
Protein	1.1 g
Fiber	0.5 g
Calories from fat	47%

Green Tea Cookies

Matcha is a powdered, brilliant emerald green tea used in Japanese tea ceremonies and to dye and flavor foods such as mochi and soba noodles. It also contains the highest concentration of antioxidants, chlorophyll, vitamins and minerals of any beverage; twice the antioxidants of red wine and approximately 9 times the beta carotene of spinach. The best part is you don't have to steep and drink it to reap its benefits; adding it to a soft sugar cookie gives them a mild green tea flavor as well as a nutritional boost.

Preheat the oven to 350°F.

In a large bowl, beat the butter, oil, sugar and green tea powder until well blended. The mixture will have the consistency of wet sand. Add the egg and vanilla and beat for a minute, until smooth and light.

Add the flour, baking powder and salt and stir by hand just until you have a soft dough.

Roll the dough into walnut-sized balls and place about two inches apart on a cookie sheet sprayed with non-stick spray. Press an almond slice, or a few, arranging them to resemble a flower, onto the top of each cookie.

Bake for 13–15 minutes, until just set and the almonds are slightly golden. Transfer to a wire rack to cool.

Makes 1½ dozen cookies.

Ingredients

¼ cup butter, softened
1 Tbsp canola or olive oil
¾ cup sugar
1 tsp dry matcha green tea powder
1 large egg
1 tsp vanilla or almond extract
1½ cups all-purpose flour
1 tsp baking powder
¼ tsp salt
sliced almonds, for decorating (optional)

Nutrition Facts
Per cookie

Calories	105
Fat	3.7 g
Saturated	1.7 g
Monounsaturated	1.3 g
Polyunsaturated	0.4 g
Carbohydrates	16.4 g
Cholesterol	19 mg
Protein	1.5 g
Fiber	0.3 g
Calories from fat	32%

Fortune Cookies

These are time consuming but a riot to make, especially since you get to create your own fortunes. They're great for parties or weddings, and larger fortune cookies with paper money tucked inside make great gifts for kids. (Just fold the bills inside a piece of paper first for hygienic reasons.)

Preheat the oven to 400°F. Get everything ready before you start. You'll have to work quickly when the cookies come out of the oven. You'll need a clean, flat surface (I use a wooden cutting board), and an empty rimless mixing bowl to shape the cookies on. Generously spray a cookie sheet with non-stick spray.

In a medium bowl, whisk together the egg and vanilla until foamy. Add the flour, sugar and salt and mix until you have a smooth thin batter.

Place a spoonful of batter into the middle of the sheet. Tilt the sheet around to make the batter run into a circle about 3 inches in diameter. (This might take a little practice, but you'll get it!) You can use a spatula to even it out if you like.

When the circle is even, place the sheet in the oven for about 5 minutes, until golden around the edges but still pale in the middle.

With a wide, thin spatula, quickly slide the cookie off the sheet and onto your work surface, flipping it upside down. Lay the fortune on the cookie, just off the center. Fold the cookie in half. The fortune should be lying along the fold, inside the cookie.

Quickly pick up the cookie and place the middle of the folded edge on the rim of the empty bowl, keeping it upright, like a taco. Pull one end down one side and the other end down the other. Hold it for a few seconds until it firms up, then transfer to a wire rack to cool completely

Ingredients

1 large egg white
¼ tsp vanilla
¼ cup all-purpose flour
¼ cup sugar
pinch salt

Nutrition Facts

Per cookie

Calories	22
Fat	0 g
Carbohydrates	5 g
Cholesterol	0 mg
Protein	0.4 g
Fiber	0.1 g
Calories from fat	0%

Once you get the hang of it, you can work with two sheets at a time, baking one cookie as you shape another. Make sure you cool the sheets in between batches.

Makes 15 cookies.

Chocolate Fortune Cookies
Replace 1 Tbsp of the flour with cocoa. Nutritional value remains the same.

Almond Macaroons

These cookies are more refined than most. I mean that in a hoity-toity sense, rather than as a reference to sugar. They're the sort you see at high-end pastry shops, and I picture well-dressed ladies holding their tea saucers in the afternoon. Almonds are an excellent source of calcium, as well as magnesium and potassium. Just a small handful contains as much calcium as 4 oz of milk, and 1 oz contains 2 grams of fiber, the same as an apple or orange.

Preheat the oven to 400°F, and line a cookie sheet with parchment, foil or a silicone mat.

In a medium bowl, stir together the ground almonds, sugar and egg whites until you have a smooth, stiff dough. Roll into walnut-sized balls and place about an inch apart on the prepared sheet.

Press a whole almond into each cookie and bake for 10–12 minutes, until just barely golden around the edges. Transfer to a wire rack to cool.

Makes 2 dozen macaroons.

Ingredients

1⅓ cups almonds, finely ground
1 cup sugar
2 large egg whites
2 dozen whole almonds

Nutrition Facts
Per cookie

Calories	118
Fat	7.4 g
Saturated	0.7 g
Monounsaturated	4.8 g
Polyunsaturated	0.6 g
Carbohydrates	11.3 g
Cholesterol	0 mg
Protein	3.1 g
Fiber	1 g
Calories from fat	54%

Ingredients

½ cup butter, softened
½ cup mild (not extra-virgin) olive or canola oil
½ cup oats (old-fashioned or quick, but not instant)
1 cup all-purpose flour
½ cup whole wheat flour
½ cup packed brown sugar
¼ cup wheat bran, oat bran or ground flaxseed (or a combination of the three)
½ tsp baking powder
¼ tsp salt

Nutrition Facts

Per wedge

Calories	128
Fat	8.6 g
Saturated	3 g
Monounsaturated	4.5 g
Polyunsaturated	0.6 g
Protein	1.3 g
Carbohydrates	12 g
Cholesterol	10.4 mg
Fiber	1 g
Calories from fat	59%

Multigrain Shortbread

The only cookie recipe noticeably absent in this book's first edition was for shortbread. There's a reason for that: shortbread is a meticulous ratio of fat, flour and sugar, and you can't mess with it without turning it into something that isn't shortbread. Because there are only 3 elements, there's nowhere for other stuff to hide, and because it has to stand on its own, back in the '90s I preferred not to mess with it. In recent years, though, I became determined to come up with shortbread every bit as tender and buttery—but with healthier fats and a boost of fiber as well. My solution involves blending butter and olive or canola oil, then re-chilling it to firm it up (ever put a bottle of olive oil in the fridge until it gets cloudy and semi-solid?) before adding it to the dry ingredients. It's still high in fat, but mostly of the healthy kind that we want to include in our diets. Eat up!

In a medium bowl, stir together the butter and oil until well blended and smooth. Put in the fridge to chill for at least an hour, or for up to several days.

When you're ready to bake, preheat the oven to 300°F.

Place the oats in the bowl of a food processor and pulse until they're as coarsely or finely ground as you like. Add the flour, whole wheat flour, brown sugar, wheat bran, baking powder and salt and pulse to combine them.

Add the chilled butter-oil mixture (it should be solid, but not quite as hard as butter) and pulse until the mixture starts to pull away from the sides of the bowl and resembles dough. Divide the dough in half and press each half into an 8-inch round cake pan. If you have only one pan, bake the shortbread in two batches, shape it into a free-form circle on an ungreased cookie sheet, or wrap the second half of dough and pop it in the fridge or freezer for another time.

Prick the dough a few times with a fork and press all around the edge of the dough with the tines of the fork to make a border. Bake the shortbread for 30–35 minutes, until it's just barely golden around the edges. Cool it in the pan for 5 minutes before cutting each circle into 12 wedges.

Pecan-Praline Shortbread
Add ½ cup finely chopped pecans to the dough along with the flour mixture. Adds 1.5 g fat, but only the good kind.

Lemon Multigrain Shortbread
Add the grated zest of a lemon along with the butter-oil mixture. Fat content remains the same.

Rosemary Shortbread
Add 1 Tbsp chopped fresh rosemary to the dough along with the flour mixture. Fat content remains the same.

Orange Chocolate Chip Shortbread
Add the grated zest of an orange along with the butter mixture, and stir in about ½ cup chopped chocolate or mini chocolate chips by hand at the end. Adds 1.3 g fat per wedge.

Old-Fashioned Sour Cream Sugar Cookies

Sometimes the simplest cookies are the most delicious. These soft, plain cookies are soft and friendly with a slightly crunchy, sugary coating.

Preheat the oven to 350°F.

In a large bowl, beat the butter and sugar until well combined. The mixture will have the consistency of wet sand. Beat in the egg and vanilla until smooth.

In a medium bowl, stir together the flour, baking soda and salt. Add half the flour mixture to the sugar mixture, stirring just until combined. Gently stir in the sour cream, and then the remaining flour mixture, stirring just until blended.

Put some sugar in a shallow dish. Drop spoonfuls of dough into the sugar and gently roll them back and forth to coat all over. Place about 2 inches apart on a cookie sheet sprayed with non-stick spray.

Bake for 12–15 minutes, until set but not yet golden. Transfer to a wire rack to cool.

Makes 1½ dozen cookies.

Sour Cream Snickerdoodles
Add 1 tsp cinnamon to the flour mixture, and ½ tsp cinnamon to the dish of sugar before rolling cookies.

Ingredients

¼ cup butter or non-hydrogenated margarine, softened
¾ cup sugar
1 large egg
1 tsp vanilla
½ cup low-fat sour cream
1½ cups all-purpose flour
½ tsp baking soda
¼ tsp salt
sugar, for rolling

Nutrition Facts
Per cookie

Calories	110
Fat	3.3 g
Saturated	1.9 g
Monounsaturated	0.9 g
Polyunsaturated	0.2 g
Carbohydrates	18.5 g
Cholesterol	20 mg
Protein	1.8 g
Fiber	0.3 g
Calories from fat	27%

LEFT TO RIGHT: Oatmeal Chocolate Chip
Cookies p. 35; Old-Fashioned Sour Cream Sugar
Cookies p. 74; Triple Chocolate Chunk Cookies p. 40

Chocolate, Pecan & Olive Oil Wafers

I came up with these for my dad, who is watching his saturated fat intake, and my mom, who is diabetic, for Christmas one year. They're very low in sugar, partly because some of it is sprinkled on top, putting its flavor and crunch at the forefront, but particularly if you don't sprinkle them with sugar at all. Because all the fat comes from the pecans and olive oil, these are especially heart-healthy.

Preheat the oven to 400°F.

In a large bowl, combine the flour, pecans, cocoa, sugar, flaxseed, baking powder and salt. In a small bowl, stir together the oil and water with a fork. Add to the dry ingredients and mix until combined.

Take walnut-sized pieces of dough and place between two pieces of waxed or parchment paper; roll back and forth in one direction with a rolling pin into large, thin ovals that look like a smear. Transfer to a cookie sheet and peel off the top sheet of paper; alternatively you could place the balls of dough directly on the sheet, cover them with a piece of parchment and roll them out, then peel off the parchment.

Stir the egg white with a fork and brush the cookies with it, then sprinkle with sugar. Bake for 8–10 minutes, until golden around the edges (it will be tough to tell!) and set. Transfer to a wire rack to cool.

Makes about 18 large cookies.

Ingredients

1⅓ cups all-purpose flour
½ cup pecans, finely chopped
⅓ cup cocoa
3–4 Tbsp sugar
1 Tbsp ground flaxseed
    (optional)
1 tsp baking powder
¼ tsp salt
½ cup olive or canola oil
¼ cup plus 2 Tbsp cold water
1 large egg white
extra sugar, for sprinkling
    (optional)

Nutrition Facts
Per cookie

Calories	119
Fat	8.2 g
Saturated	1 g
Monounsaturated	5.7 g
Polyunsaturated	1 g
Carbohydrates	10.7 g
Cholesterol	0 mg
Fiber	1.2 g
Calories from fat	60%

Espresso Bean Cookies

These were inspired by some wonderful espresso shortbread cookies I bought on a ski hill that were shaped like coffee beans. Of course, being shortbread they held their shape, but were ludicrously high in fat; after we polished them off the bag they came in was soaked with butter. These are much lower in fat, softer and chewier so they don't hold their coffee bean shape after baking, but you can still see the subtle imprint down the middle. Of course, you can skip this step entirely if you want.

In a large bowl, beat the butter, oil, sugar and espresso powder until well blended. The mixture will have the consistency of wet sand. Add the egg and vanilla and beat for a minute, until smooth and light.

Add the flour, baking powder and salt and stir by hand just until you have a soft dough. Wrap the dough in plastic wrap and refrigerate for about an hour, or overnight.

When ready to bake, preheat the oven to 350°F. Roll the chilled dough into 1½-inch balls, then roll between your palms to make into ovals and place about an inch apart on a cookie sheet sprayed with non-stick spray. Press a chopstick or the handle of a wooden spoon lengthwise into the dough to make a deep imprint, so that they resemble big coffee beans.

Bake for 12–15 minutes, until they've spread a bit and turned slightly golden around the edges. Transfer to a wire rack to cool.

Makes 1½ dozen cookies.

Chocolate Mocha Coffee Beans

Replace ¼ cup of the flour with cocoa powder. Nutritional value remains the same.

Ingredients

¼ cup butter, softened
1 Tbsp canola oil
¾ cup sugar
1 Tbsp instant espresso or
    coffee powder
1 large egg
1 tsp vanilla
1½ cups all-purpose flour
1 tsp baking powder
¼ tsp salt

Nutrition Facts
Per cookie

Calories	105
Fat	3.7 g
Saturated	1.7 g
Monounsaturated	1.3 g
Polyunsaturated	0.4 g
Carbohydrates	16.4 g
Cholesterol	19 mg
Protein	1.5 g
Fiber	0.3 g
Calories from fat	32%

Ingredients

¼ cup butter or non-hydrogenated margarine, softened
1 cup sugar
1 large egg
1 Tbsp milk
1 tsp vanilla
1 cup flour
1 tsp baking powder
¼ tsp salt
2 cups corn flakes
½ cup chocolate chips, chopped dried fruit, chopped nuts or a combination (optional)

Nutrition Facts
Per cookie

Calories	137
Fat	2.9 g
Saturated	1.7 g
Monounsaturated	0.9 g
Polyunsaturated	0.2 g
Carbohydrates	25.6 g
Cholesterol	19 mg
Protein	1.9 g
Fiber	0.5 g
Calories from fat	19%

Corn Flake Cookies

Corn flakes make these buttery cookies crunchy, and like oats, go very well with chewy bits of dried fruit, chopped nuts, chocolate or butterscotch chips.

Preheat the oven to 375°F.

In a large bowl, beat the butter and sugar with an electric mixer for a minute, until fluffy. Beat in the egg, milk and vanilla until smooth.

Add the flour, baking powder and salt and stir by hand until almost combined; add corn flakes and any other additions you like and stir just until blended.

Roll the dough into walnut-sized balls and place them about an inch apart on a cookie sheet sprayed with non-stick spray. Bake for 12–15 minutes, until very pale golden and still soft in the middle. Transfer to a wire rack to cool.

Makes 1½ dozen cookies.

LEFT TO RIGHT: Bull's-Eyes p. 105;
Cinnamon Sugar Phyllo Twists p. 59;
Corn Flake Cookies p. 78

Ingredients

Cookies

3 Tbsp butter or non-hydrogenated margarine, softened
1 cup sugar
1 large egg
1 tsp vanilla
2 cups all-purpose flour
½ cup cocoa
½ tsp salt
1 tsp baking soda
½ cup buttermilk
½ cup chocolate chips

Filling

1 jar marshmallow cream

Nutrition Facts

Per cookie

Calories	288
Fat	6.6 g
Saturated	3.8 g
Monounsaturated	1.8 g
Polyunsaturated	0.6 g
Carbohydrates	55 g
Cholesterol	26.8 mg
Protein	4.7 g
Fiber	3 g
Calories from fat	20%

Whoopie Pies

Remember Jos. Louis cakes—those big chocolate sandwich cakes with whipped cream filling? As a kid I'd spend my allowance on them. These are essentially the same thing—huge cakey cookies sandwiched with jarred marshmallow cream, or frozen and made into ice cream sandwiches with light vanilla ice cream. Of course, they'll never replicate the packaged experience, but they really do taste better, are so much better for you, and cheaper, too.

Preheat the oven to 375°F.

In a large bowl, beat the butter and sugar for a minute or so, until well combined. It will have the consistency of wet sand. Add the egg and vanilla and beat until smooth.

In a medium bowl, stir together the flour, cocoa and salt. In a small bowl, stir the baking soda into ½ cup very hot water until dissolved.

With the mixer on low, add half the flour mixture, then half the buttermilk, then half the baking soda mixture, mixing each time just until blended. Repeat with the remaining flour mixture, buttermilk and baking soda mixture, mixing just until combined. Stir in the chocolate chips. The batter will be quite wet, almost like cake batter.

Drop large, round spoonfuls of batter 2 inches apart on a cookie sheet sprayed with non-stick spray. (If you're making pies, try to keep the mounds similar in size and shape so that they'll make even sandwiches). Bake for 12–15 minutes, until the tops no longer appear wet and just spring back when lightly touched. Transfer cookies to a wire rack to cool.

When completely cool, spread the bottom of one cookie with marshmallow cream, then sandwich with a second cookie. Repeat with remaining cookies and cream. Store extras, individually wrapped, in plastic wrap.

Makes 1 dozen pies or 2 dozen cookies.

Ice Cream Sandwiches

Freeze cookies in a single layer on a cookie sheet. Spread one cookie with softened light ice cream, orange sherbet or frozen yogurt (instead of marshmallow cream); top with a second cookie, wrap individually in plastic wrap and freeze.

Rolled Sugar Cookies

Butter Pecan Diamonds

Chocolate Cream Cheese Sandwich Cookies

Crunchy Raisin Sandwich Cookies

Peppermint Patties

Linzer Cookies

Butterscotch Crunch Cookies

Gingersnaps

Rolled Cookies

Ingredients

¼ cup butter, softened
1 Tbsp canola oil
¾ cup sugar
grated zest of 1 lemon
    (optional)
1 large egg
1 tsp vanilla
1⅔ cups all-purpose flour
1 tsp baking powder
¼ tsp salt

Nutrition Facts

Per cookie

Calories	54
Fat	1.9 g
Saturated	0.9 g
Monounsaturated	0.7 g
Polyunsaturated	0.2 g
Carbohydrates	8.6 g
Cholesterol	9.4 mg
Protein	0.8 g
Fiber	0.2 g
Calories from fat	31%

Rolled Sugar Cookies

This is a great basic cookie dough to start with; you can add spices and other flavorings such as grated lemon or orange zest or various extracts to customize them if you like. It's important when you make rolled cookies to handle the dough as little as possible, and gently re-roll any scraps only once. Handling the dough too much develops the gluten, making your cookies tough.

In a large bowl, beat the butter, oil, sugar and lemon zest with an electric mixer until well combined. Add the egg and vanilla and beat for a minute, until smooth and light.

In a small bowl, stir together the flour, baking powder and salt. Add to the sugar mixture and stir by hand just until you have a soft dough. Shape the dough into a disc, wrap in plastic and refrigerate for an hour or until well chilled.

When you're ready to bake, preheat the oven to 350°F. Roll the dough out between two sheets of waxed paper or on a surface very lightly dusted with a combination of flour and sugar until it's ⅛–¼-inch thick. Cut out cookies using a 2–3-inch cookie cutter or glass rim. Re-roll the scraps once to get as many cookies as possible.

Place the cookies an inch apart on a cookie sheet sprayed with non-stick spray. Bake for 10–12 minutes, until pale golden around the edges. Transfer to a wire rack to cool.

Makes 3 dozen cookies.

Orange Sugar Cookies with Chocolate

Substitute grated orange zest for the lemon zest. Place ¾ cup chocolate chips in a zip-lock bag, seal and place in a bowl of very warm water to melt. When the cookies have cooled and the chocolate has melted (knead it with your fingers to make sure there are no bits left), snip a tiny hole in one corner of the bag. Drizzle the cookies with melted chocolate by squeezing the bag. Adds 1 g fat per cookie.

Lemon Poppy Seed Sugar Cookies

Include the lemon zest and add 2 Tbsp poppy seeds to the sugar mixture. Mix and bake as directed. Fat content remains the same. These are great sandwiched with Lemon Cream Cheese Frosting (page 198).

Chocolate Sugar Cookies

Replace ½ cup of the flour with cocoa. Fat content remains the same.

Tiny Lemon Curd Sandwiches

Cut rolled-out dough into rounds with a 1¼-inch cookie cutter. Spread baked, cooled cookies with lemon curd, sandwich with a second cookie and sprinkle with icing sugar. Added fat depends on the type of lemon curd you use.

Ingredients

1¾ cups sugar
¾ cup finely chopped pecans
¼ cup butter, softened
1 tsp vanilla
1 large egg
1 large egg white
2 cups all-purpose flour
1 tsp baking powder
¼ tsp salt
½ cup chocolate chips, for
    drizzling (optional)

Nutrition Facts

Per cookie

Calories	110
Fat	3.6 g
Saturated	1.2 g
Monounsaturated	1.7 g
Polyunsaturated	0.6 g
Carbohydrates	18.6 g
Cholesterol	11.3 mg
Protein	1.4 g
Fiber	0.4 g
Calories from fat	29%

Butter Pecan Diamonds

There's something about cookies with a sugary surface that's instantly appealing; maybe it's that the sugar is right there for all to see, or that it's the first thing you taste, and you get sugary lips. Cutting these with a knife is easier than using a cookie cutter or glass rim: you avoid having any scraps to re-roll (any edge scraps can be baked along with the cookies and snacked on later), and their diamond shape makes them look particularly noble.

Preheat the oven to 350°F.

In a large bowl, stir together the sugar and pecans. Remove ¾ cup of the mixture and set aside. Add the butter, vanilla, egg and egg white to the remaining sugar mixture and beat until creamy and well blended.

Add the flour, baking powder and salt and stir by hand just until you have a soft dough. On a lightly floured surface or between two sheets of waxed or parchment paper, roll the dough into a 12- × 18-inch rectangle. Sprinkle evenly with the reserved sugar-pecan mixture and roll gently with the rolling pin to help sugar adhere to the dough.

With a knife or pizza wheel, cut the dough diagonally into 2-inch strips, then cut the same way in the opposite direction, forming diamonds. Place 1–2 inches apart on a cookie sheet sprayed with non-stick spray.

Bake for 12–15 minutes, until pale golden around the edges. Transfer to a wire rack to cool. If you want to drizzle them with chocolate, put the chocolate chips in a zip-lock bag, seal and place in a bowl of very warm water to melt. When the chocolate has melted (knead it with your fingers to make sure there are no bits left), snip a tiny hole in one corner of the bag and drizzle the cookies with chocolate by squeezing the bag.

Makes 2½ dozen cookies.

Chocolate Cream Cheese Sandwich Cookies

These make great chocolate cookies whether you turn them into sandwiches or not: left plain, they are fantastic dunked in milk, smeared with frosting, sandwiched with ice cream or dipped in melted chocolate. Substitute any kind of frosting for the cream cheese filling.

In a large bowl, beat together the butter, sugar and brown sugar until well combined. It will have the consistency of wet sand. Add the egg, coffee and vanilla and beat until smooth and light.

In a medium bowl, stir together the flour, cocoa, baking soda and salt, making sure to break up any lumps of cocoa. Add to the sugar mixture and stir by hand just until the dough comes together. Shape into a disc, wrap in plastic wrap or waxed paper and refrigerate for an hour or up to a week.

When ready to bake, preheat the oven to 350°F. On a lightly floured surface or between two sheets of waxed paper, roll the dough about ⅛ inch thick and cut into 2–2¼-inch rounds with a cookie cutter or into squares with a knife. Re-roll the scraps once to get as many cookies as you can and place about an inch apart on an ungreased cookie sheet.

Bake for 10–12 minutes, until set. Transfer to a wire rack to cool.

To make the filling, beat the cream cheese in a medium bowl with an electric mixer until fluffy. Beat in the icing sugar, water and vanilla, adding a little more sugar or water as needed until you have a spreadable frosting. Spread half the cooled cookies with icing and top with a second cookie.

Makes 20 sandwich cookies.

Ingredients

Cookies
¼ cup butter, softened
½ cup sugar
½ cup packed brown sugar
1 large egg
1 tsp instant coffee powder, dissolved in 1 Tbsp water
1 tsp vanilla
1 cup all-purpose flour
½ cup cocoa
¼ tsp baking soda
¼ tsp salt

Filling
¼ cup light cream cheese (plain or strawberry)
1½ cups icing sugar
1 Tbsp water or milk
¼ tsp vanilla

Nutrition Facts
Per cookie

Calories	133
Fat	3.4 g
Saturated	1.9 g
Monounsaturated	1 g
Polyunsaturated	0.2 g
Carbohydrates	25.5 g
Cholesterol	18.8 mg
Protein	1.7 g
Fiber	1.2 g
Calories from fat	22%

Ingredients

Cookies

3 Tbsp butter, softened
⅓ cup sugar
2 cups all-purpose flour
½ tsp baking powder
¼ tsp salt
½ cup milk
2 cups chopped dried fruit
   such as raisins, apricots,
   dates, cranberries or
   cherries

Glaze

2 Tbsp milk
2 Tbsp sugar

Nutrition Facts

Per cookie

Calories	98
Fat	1.7 g
Saturated	1 g
Monounsaturated	0.5 g
Polyunsaturated	0.1 g
Carbohydrates	19.8 g
Cholesterol	4 mg
Protein	1.7 g
Fiber	1.2 g
Calories from fat	15%

Crunchy Raisin Sandwich Cookies

Don't let the long instructions scare you off. These are quite simple and very satisfying to make. It's an adaptation of a recipe from Maida Heatter's Brand-New Book of Great Cookies, *and they're truly great cookies: crunchy, plain, not too sweet — not usually selling points for me, but they're one of my all-time favorites.*

In a large bowl, beat together the butter and sugar until creamy. In a small bowl, stir together the flour, baking powder and salt. Add the flour mixture to the sugar mixture in three additions, alternating with the milk in two additions, beginning and ending with the flour. Stir by hand just until combined.

Gather up the dough with your hands and transfer it to a lightly floured surface. Shape the dough into a 4- × 8-inch rectangle, wrap in plastic and refrigerate for an hour.

When chilled, remove the dough from the fridge, cut in half to make two squares and return half to the fridge. On a lightly floured surface, roll the first piece out to make a 9-inch square, keeping the edges as straight as possible.

Line a cookie sheet with parchment or waxed paper, and transfer the rolled dough onto the sheet. Sprinkle the fruit evenly over the dough, so that it comes right to the edges. Roll the second piece of dough to the same size as the first; transfer it carefully on top of the dried fruit. With the rolling pin, roll the dough to press it securely together, and to make a 12-inch square. The fruit will almost come through the top layer of dough — that's okay!

Press against the edges with a ruler or dough scraper to keep them straight. Cover the dough with plastic wrap and place in the freezer for an hour or overnight.

When ready to bake, preheat the oven to 375°F. Remove the pan from the freezer and with a large sharp knife, cut the dough into quarters. If you want very neat squares, trim the edges. The scraps may be baked along with the cut cookies. Cut each quarter into 3 strips, then cut across in half to make 6 rectangular bars.

As you cut the first two quarters, place the bars 1 inch apart on an ungreased cookie sheet. Brush the tops of the cookies with milk, and sprinkle them with sugar. Bake for 20–25 minutes, or until pale golden around the edges. Transfer to a wire rack to cool. Repeat with the remaining cookie dough.

Makes 2 dozen cookies.

Ingredients

¼ cup butter, softened
1 Tbsp canola oil
¾ cup sugar
1 large egg
1 tsp peppermint extract
1¼ cups all-purpose flour
½ cup cocoa
1 tsp baking powder
¼ tsp salt
½ cup mint chocolate chips
  (optional)

Nutrition Facts

Per cookie

Calories	62
Fat	2.3 g
Saturated	1.1 g
Monounsaturated	0.8 g
Polyunsaturated	0.2 g
Carbohydrates	10 g
Cholesterol	11.3 mg
Protein	1.1 g
Fiber	0.8 g
Calories from fat	32%

Peppermint Patties

A mild addiction to those mint cookies the Girl Guides sell every fall prompted me to come up with some of my own. Dipping them in or drizzling them with melted mint chocolate chips makes them more authentic, but they're equally delicious naked.

In a large bowl, beat the butter, oil and sugar with an electric mixer until well combined. Add egg and mint extract and beat for a minute, until smooth and light.

In a small bowl, stir together the flour, cocoa, baking powder and salt. Add to the sugar mixture and stir by hand just until you have a soft dough. Shape the dough into a disc, wrap in plastic and refrigerate for an hour or until well chilled.

When you're ready to bake, preheat the oven to 350°F. Roll the dough out between two sheets of waxed paper or on a surface very lightly dusted with a combination of flour and sugar until it's ⅛–¼-inch thick. Cut out cookies using a 2-inch cookie cutter, or cut into squares with a knife. Re-roll the scraps once to get as many cookies as possible.

Place the cookies an inch apart on a cookie sheet sprayed with non-stick spray. Bake for 10–12 minutes, until set. Transfer to a wire rack to cool.

To melt the chocolate chips, put them in a zip-lock bag, seal and place in a bowl of very warm water to melt. When the cookies have cooled and the chocolate has melted (knead it with your fingers to make sure there are no bits left), snip a tiny hole in one corner of the bag. Drizzle the cookies with melted chocolate by squeezing the bag.

Makes 2½ dozen cookies.

Linzer Cookies

Linzer cookies were created by an Austrian baker, Herr Linzer, as an anniversary gift for his wife, Heidi. They're beautiful and perfect to package up to give away, shaped as hearts, stars or whatever you like.

Preheat the oven to 350°F.

Roll the cookie dough out ¼ inch thick between two sheets of waxed paper or on a surface lightly dusted with flour and sugar. Cut out cookies using a 2–3-inch round cookie cutter or glass rim. Using a small (½-inch) round or shaped cutter, cut the centers out of half the cookies. Re-roll the scraps once to get as many cookies as possible.

Transfer the cookies to a cookie sheet sprayed with non-stick spray, and sprinkle the cookies with the cut-out centers with almonds, if using, pressing gently to help them stick.

Bake for 10–12 minutes, until pale golden around the edges. Transfer to a wire rack to cool. Spread the solid cookies with jam, and sprinkle the cut-out cookies lightly with icing sugar, shaking it through a fine sieve if you have one. Top each jam-covered cookie with a cut-out cookie.

Makes 1½ dozen sandwich cookies.

Cherry or Mincemeat Turnovers

Cut cookie dough into 3-inch rounds and place on the prepared cookie sheet. Make a cherry filling by mixing ⅔ cup cherry preserves with ½ cup chopped dried cherries (or use apricot preserves and dried apricots, or peach preserves and dried peaches). Place about a teaspoon of fruit filling or jarred mincemeat in the middle of each round, and fold over to form a pocket, like a perogy. Press the edges with a fork to seal, and poke the top once or twice. Bake for 12–15 minutes, until pale golden. Transfer to a wire rack to cool, and then sprinkle with icing sugar.

Ingredients

1 batch Rolled Sugar Cookie
   dough (page 84)
Filling & Topping
⅓ cup raspberry or apricot jam
½ cup sliced almonds
   (optional)
icing sugar, for sprinkling
   (optional)

Nutrition Facts
Per cookie

Calories	123
Fat	3.7 g
Saturated	1.8 g
Monounsaturated	1.3 g
Polyunsaturated	0.4 g
Carbohydrates	21 g
Cholesterol	19 mg
Protein	1.6 g
Fiber	0.4 g
Calories from fat	27%

Ingredients

¼ cup butter, softened
1 Tbsp canola oil
¾ cup packed brown sugar
1 large egg
1 tsp vanilla
1¾ cups flour
1 tsp baking powder
¼ tsp salt
½ cup crushed hard
    butterscotch candy (such
    as Werther's Original or
    Life Savers)

Nutrition Facts

Per cookie

Calories	90
Fat	2.5 g
Saturated	1.3 g
Monounsaturated	0.8 g
Polyunsaturated	0.2 g
Carbohydrates	15.7 g
Cholesterol	14.3 mg
Protein	1.2 g
Fiber	0.3 g
Calories from fat	25%

Butterscotch Crunch Cookies

Fans of butterscotch, this is the cookie for you. It's a brown sugar dough, studded with nubs of butterscotch and baked until crunchy. A regular roll of butterscotch Life Savers works perfectly. To crush them, empty into a zip-lock bag and bash with the bottom of a wine bottle or roll with a rolling pin.

In a large bowl, beat the butter, oil and brown sugar until well combined. Add the egg and vanilla and beat for a minute, until smooth and fluffy.

In a small bowl, stir together the flour, baking powder and salt. Add the flour mixture and crushed candy to the sugar mixture and stir by hand just until you have a soft dough. Shape the dough into a disc, wrap in plastic and refrigerate for an hour or up to a few days.

When you're ready to bake, preheat the oven to 350°F. Unwrap the dough and roll it out to about ⅛ inch thick between two sheets of waxed paper or on a surface lightly dusted with flour and sugar.

Cut out cookies using a 2–2½-inch cookie cutter or glass rim. Transfer to a cookie sheet that has been sprayed with non-stick spray. Re-roll the scraps once to get as many cookies as possible.

Bake for 10–12 minutes, until pale golden around the edges. Transfer to a wire rack to cool.

Makes 2 dozen cookies.

Butterscotch Crunch Icebox Cookies

Press the dough into an 8- × 4-inch loaf tin lined with plastic wrap or aluminum foil. Freeze, then remove the brick and wrap well; freeze for 3 hours or up to 3 months. To bake, slice ¼ inch thick and bake as directed.

Gingersnaps

Gingersnaps are meant to be nice and thin—the thinner the cookie, the more "snappy" they are—and can be as spicy or mild as you like. Add extra spice if you see fit, or a good grinding of fresh black pepper. If you want to use fresh ginger, add it to the butter-sugar mixture.

In a large bowl, beat the butter and brown sugar until light and fluffy. Add the molasses and egg and beat until smooth.

In a medium bowl, combine the flour, baking soda, cinnamon, ginger, allspice and salt. Add to the sugar mixture and stir by hand just until blended. Divide the dough in half, shape each piece into a disc, wrap in plastic and refrigerate for 2 hours or up to a few days.

When you're ready to bake, preheat the oven to 350°F. Roll one piece of dough at a time between two sheets of waxed or parchment paper or on a surface lightly dusted with flour and sugar to about ⅛ thick. Cut into rounds or 2-inch squares with a knife, pizza cutter or crimped pastry wheel. Transfer to a cookie sheet sprayed with non-stick spray, and prick each cookie a few times with a fork.

Bake for 10–12 minutes, until crisp. Cool completely on a wire rack.

Makes about 4 dozen cookies.

Ingredients

¼ cup butter, softened
⅓ cup packed brown sugar
⅓ cup dark molasses
1 large egg
2 cups all-purpose flour
1 tsp baking soda
½–1 tsp cinnamon
½ tsp ground ginger
¼ tsp allspice
¼ tsp salt

Nutrition Facts
Per cookie

Calories	41
Fat	1.1 g
Saturated	0.6 g
Monounsaturated	0.3 g
Polyunsaturated	0.1 g
Carbohydrates	7 g
Cholesterol	7 mg
Protein	0.7 g
Fiber	0.2 g
Calories from fat	24%

Icebox Sugar Cookies

Chocolate Icebox Sugar Cookies

Peanut Butter Crunch Icebox Cookies

Chocolate Peanut Butter Ribbons

Marmalade Hazelnut Swirls

Spiced Whole Wheat Date Spirals

Bull's-Eyes

Cinnamon Bun Crunch Icebox Cookies

Icebox Cookies

Ingredients

¼ cup butter or non-hydrogenated margarine, softened
⅔ cup sugar
1 large egg white or 1 large
   egg
2 tsp vanilla
1¼ cups flour
¼ tsp baking soda
¼ tsp salt

Nutrition Facts
Per cookie

Calories	64
Fat	2 g
Saturated	1.2 g
Monounsaturated	0.6 g
Polyunsaturated	0.1 g
Carbohydrates	10.6 g
Cholesterol	5.2 mg
Protein	0.8 g
Fiber	0.2 g
Calories from fat	28%

Icebox Sugar Cookies

This basic sugar cookie dough is versatile. You can add chopped dried fruit, nuts, candies and chocolate, or flavor the dough with grated citrus zest, spices or different extracts. Because icebox cookie doughs are so similar, they can be mixed and matched and baked together; try swirling or shaping contrasting icebox cookie doughs to create interesting effects.

In a large bowl, beat the butter and sugar with an electric mixer until well combined. Add the egg white and vanilla and beat until smooth.

Add the flour, baking soda and salt and stir by hand just until you have a soft dough. Gather the dough into a ball, shape into a 6-inch log, wrap in waxed paper or plastic wrap and freeze for at least 3 hours, or up to 3 months.

When you're ready to bake, preheat the oven to 350°F. With a sharp knife, slice the frozen log into ¼-inch slices and place about an inch apart on a cookie sheet sprayed with non-stick spray. Bake for 8–10 minutes, until barely golden. Transfer cookies to a wire rack to cool.

Makes 2 dozen cookies.

Chocolate Chip Icebox Cookies

Use half white sugar and half packed brown sugar, and add 1 cup coarsely chopped chocolate chips and ½ cup chopped walnuts or pecans along with the flour mixture. Adds 2 g fat per cookie.

Citrus Icebox Cookies

Add the grated zest of a lemon and an orange to the butter-sugar mixture. As soon as the cookies come out of the oven, dip them in icing sugar to coat completely, then set on a wire rack to cool. Fat content remains the same.

Maple Walnut Icebox Cookies

Use packed brown sugar instead of white, and maple extract instead of vanilla. Add ½ cup finely chopped toasted walnuts to the dough before shaping into a log. Adds 1.5 g fat per cookie, but only the good kind.

Ginger Hazelnut Icebox Cookies

Add 1 Tbsp grated fresh ginger to the butter-sugar mixture, and stir ½ cup chopped toasted hazelnuts into the dough along with the flour. Adds 1.7 g fat per cookie, but only the good kind.

Ingredients

¼ cup butter or non-hydroge-
    nated margarine, softened
⅔ cup sugar
1 large egg white or 1 large
    egg
2 tsp vanilla
1 cup flour
¼ cup cocoa
¼ tsp baking soda
¼ tsp salt

Nutrition Facts

Per cookie

Calories	61
Fat	2 g
Saturated	1.2 g
Monounsaturated	0.6 g
Polyunsaturated	0.1 g
Carbohydrates	10.1 g
Cholesterol	5.2 mg
Protein	1 g
Fiber	0.6 g
Calories from fat	29%

Chocolate Icebox Sugar Cookies

These simple chocolate cookies are great to have on hand in the freezer. They're wonderful with added chopped toasted nuts, chopped chocolate chips or crushed candy canes. If you like, roll the logs of dough in coarse sugar before wrapping and freezing to give your cookies a sweet, crunchy edge.

In a large bowl, beat the butter and sugar with an electric mixer until well combined. Add the egg white and vanilla and beat until smooth.

In a small bowl, stir together the flour, cocoa, baking soda and salt; add to the butter-sugar mixture and stir by hand just until you have a soft dough. Gather the dough into a ball, shape into a 6-inch log, wrap in waxed paper or plastic wrap and freeze for at least 3 hours, or up to 3 months.

When you're ready to bake, preheat the oven to 350°F. With a sharp knife, slice the frozen log into ¼-inch slices and place about an inch apart on a cookie sheet sprayed with non-stick spray. Bake for 8–10 minutes, until barely golden. Transfer cookies to a wire rack to cool.

Makes 2 dozen cookies.

Chocolate Orange Icebox Sugar Cookies

Add the grated zest of an orange to the sugar mixture while beating. Fat content remains the same.

Chocolate Gingerbread

Reduce the sugar to ½ cup and add ¼ cup molasses to the butter-sugar mixture, and ½ tsp cinnamon, ½ tsp ground ginger, ¼ tsp allspice and a pinch of ground cloves to the flour mixture. Fat content remains the same.

Black & White Striped Cookies

Start with a log of plain sugar cookie dough and a log of chocolate sugar cookie dough. Slice each log in quarters lengthwise and reassemble two logs alternating plain and chocolate dough. Roll the log on the countertop to smooth it out and help the layers adhere. Slice and bake as directed.

Ingredients

¼ cup light or regular peanut butter, smooth or crunchy

2 Tbsp butter or non-hydrogenated margarine, softened

⅓ cup sugar

⅓ cup packed brown sugar

2 large egg whites or 1 large egg

2 tsp vanilla

1⅓ cup flour

¼ tsp baking soda

¼ tsp salt

½ cup crushed peanut brittle (place in a zip-lock bag and crush with a rolling pin or hammer)

Nutrition Facts

Per cookie

Calories	98
Fat	3.1 g
Saturated	1.1 g
Monounsaturated	1.2 g
Polyunsaturated	0.7 g
Carbohydrates	16 g
Cholesterol	3.4 mg
Protein	2 g
Fiber	0.2 g
Calories from fat	26%

Peanut Butter Crunch Icebox Cookies

Lovers of peanut butter cookies need a freezer stash too; adding crushed peanut brittle gives them a whole new peanut flavor and texture dimension. (Leave it out if you don't have any.)

In a medium bowl, beat the peanut butter, butter, sugar and brown sugar until creamy. Add the egg whites and vanilla and beat until smooth. Add the flour, baking soda, salt and peanut brittle, and stir by hand just until you have a soft dough.

Shape the dough into an 8-inch log, wrap in waxed paper or plastic wrap and freeze for 3 hours or up to 3 months.

When you're ready to bake, preheat the oven to 350°F. Slice the frozen log into ¼ inch thick slices and place about an inch apart on a cookie sheet sprayed with non-stick spray. Bake for 10–12 minutes, until pale golden around the edges. Transfer to a wire rack to cool.

Makes 2 dozen cookies.

Chocolate Peanut Butter Ribbons

Most icebox cookie doughs are rolled into cylinders before they are frozen, but these are a bit different. By pressing alternating layers of contrasting dough into a loaf pan, you end up with striped cookies that are long and rectangular rather than small and round. If you don't want your loaf pan to be used as freezer storage, pull out the frozen brick of dough once it has frozen, wrap in another layer of plastic wrap and return it to the freezer on its own.

Line a 9- × 5-inch loaf pan with plastic wrap. Press half the chocolate dough evenly in the pan. Top with half the peanut butter dough, then the remaining chocolate dough and the remaining peanut butter dough, pressing each layer down firmly. Cover the top with plastic and freeze until firm. Remove the frozen dough from the pan, wrap and store in the freezer for up to 3 months.

When you're ready to bake, preheat the oven to 350°F. Let the frozen dough stand at room temperature for about 10 minutes to make it easier to cut. Unwrap the dough and place it on a cutting board. Cut the dough crosswise into thirds. Slice each third crosswise into ¼ inch thick slices and place an inch apart on a cookie sheet sprayed with non-stick spray.

Bake for 10–12 minutes, until the edges are set. Transfer to a wire rack to cool.

Makes 3 dozen cookies.

Ingredients

1 batch Chocolate Icebox
   Sugar Cookie dough
   (page 98)
1 batch Peanut Butter Crunch
   Icebox Cookie dough
   (page 100)

Nutrition Facts
Per cookie

Calories	106
Fat	3.4 g
Saturated	1.5 g
Monounsaturated	1.2 g
Polyunsaturated	0.5 g
Carbohydrates	17.5 g
Cholesterol	5.7 mg
Protein	2 g
Fiber	0.5 g
Calories from fat	28%

Ingredients

Dough

¼ cup butter or non-hydrogenated margarine, softened
⅔ cup sugar
1 large egg
2 tsp vanilla
1¼ cups flour
¼ tsp baking soda
¼ tsp salt

Filling

½ cup marmalade
⅓ cup flaked hazelnuts,
   toasted

Nutrition Facts

Per cookie

Calories	94
Fat	3.3 g
Saturated	1.4 g
Monounsaturated	1.5 g
Polyunsaturated	0.3 g
Carbohydrates	15.3 g
Cholesterol	14.2 mg
Protein	1.3 g
Fiber	0.4 g
Calories from fat	31%

Marmalade Hazelnut Swirls

There are a lot of different things you can do here: icebox swirls are most often made with raspberry jam, but experiment with other flavors. I like marmalade with hazelnuts (they come sliced or "flaked"). Use any kind of marmalade you like, or try peach or apricot jam.

In a medium bowl, beat the butter and sugar with an electric mixer for a minute, until well combined. Add the egg and vanilla and beat until smooth.

Add the flour, baking soda and salt and stir by hand just until you have a soft dough. Roll the dough between two sheets of waxed or parchment paper into a 12-inch square. Place on a cookie sheet in the fridge for about 30 minutes or in the freezer for 15 minutes, until it firms up a bit.

Remove the dough from the fridge and peel off the top layer of waxed paper. Spread the dough evenly with marmalade, going right to the edges. Sprinkle with nuts. Gently roll into a log, starting with a long edge and peeling back the bottom paper as you go. Wrap the log in the sheet of waxed paper or plastic wrap and freeze for 3 hours or up to 3 months.

When you're ready to bake, preheat the oven to 350°F. Slice the log into ¼ inch thick slices and place an inch apart on a cookie sheet sprayed with non-stick spray. Bake for 12–15 minutes, until pale golden. Let cool on the cookie sheet for a few minutes before transferring to a wire rack to cool completely.

Makes 3 dozen cookies.

Cranberry Orange Swirls

Cook ½ cup whole berry cranberry sauce, 2 Tbsp orange marmalade and 2 tsp cornstarch in a small saucepan over medium heat until the mixture comes to a boil. Set aside to cool and use as a filling instead of the marmalade and hazelnuts. Fat is reduced by 1 g per cookie.

Raspberry Swirls

Bring ½ cup raspberry jam and 1 tsp cornstarch to a boil in a small saucepan; use instead of the marmalade and hazelnuts. Fat is reduced by 1 g per cookie.

Spiced Apricot Swirls

Stir 1 tsp cinammon into ½ cup apricot jam and use as a filling instead of the marmalade and hazelnuts. Fat is reduced by 1 g per cookie.

Spiced Whole Wheat Date Spirals

These have the same flavor as date squares, unless you substitute chopped dried apricots or raisins for the dates.

In a medium saucepan, combine the dates, sugar and orange juice. Bring to a boil; reduce heat and simmer, stirring frequently, for about 5 minutes or until thick and jam-like. Set aside to cool.

In a medium bowl, beat the butter and sugar with an electric mixer for a minute, until well combined. Add the egg and vanilla and beat until smooth. In a small bowl, stir together the flour, baking soda, cinnamon, salt and allspice. Add to the sugar mixture and stir by hand just until you have a soft dough.

Roll the dough between two sheets of waxed or parchment paper into a 12-inch square. Place on a cookie sheet in the fridge for about 30 minutes or in the freezer for 15 minutes, until it firms up a bit.

Remove the dough from the fridge and peel off the top layer of waxed paper. Spread the dough evenly with the date filling, going right to the edges. Starting from a long edge, gently roll into a log, peeling back the paper as you go. Wrap the log in waxed paper or plastic wrap and freeze for 3 hours or up to 3 months.

When you're ready to bake, preheat the oven to 350°F. Slice the log into ¼ inch thick slices and place an inch apart on a cookie sheet sprayed with non-stick spray. Bake for 12–15 minutes, until pale golden. Let cool on the cookie sheet for a few minutes before transferring to a wire rack to cool.

Makes 3 dozen cookies.

Ingredients

Dough

¼ cup butter or non-hydrogenated margarine, softened
⅓ cup packed brown sugar
1 large egg
2 tsp vanilla
¾ cup whole wheat flour
½ cup all-purpose flour
¼ tsp baking soda
1 tsp cinnamon
¼ tsp salt
pinch allspice

Filling

1 cup chopped dates or figs
¼ cup sugar (white or brown)
½ cup orange juice or water

Nutrition Facts

Per cookie

Calories	66
Fat	1.5 g
Saturated	0.9 g
Monounsaturated	0.4 g
Polyunsaturated	0.1 g
Carbohydrates	13 g
Cholesterol	9.4 mg
Protein	0.8 g
Fiber	1 g
Calories from fat	20%

Whole Wheat Orange Fig Spirals

Cook 1 cup finely chopped dried figs, ⅓ cup marmalade and ¼ cup orange juice in a small saucepan over medium heat until the mixture comes to a boil. Set aside to cool and use as a filling instead of the date mixture. Fat content remains the same.

Bull's-Eyes

These look really cool and are excellent with grated orange zest added to the plain sugar cookie dough.

Divide the chocolate dough in half, and roll each half into an 8-inch log. Wrap each log in waxed paper or plastic wrap and freeze for an hour.

Meanwhile, divide the white dough in half and roll each piece into a 3- × 8-inch rectangle between two sheets of waxed or parchment paper. Remove one chocolate log from the freezer and place it on one of the rectangles of white dough; wrap the log in the dough, sealing the edges. Repeat with the remaining dough log. Wrap in waxed paper or plastic wrap and freeze for 3 hours or up to 3 months.

When you're ready to bake, preheat the oven to 350°F. Remove one log at a time from the freezer, slice into ¼ inch thick slices and place about an inch apart on a cookie sheet sprayed with non-stick spray. Bake for 10–12 minutes, until the edges are firm. Transfer to a wire rack to cool.

Makes 4 dozen cookies.

Ingredients

1 batch Chocolate Icebox Sugar Cookie dough (page 98)
1 batch Icebox Sugar Cookie dough (page 96) or Peanut Butter Crunch Icebox Cookie dough (page 100)

Nutrition Facts
Per cookie

Calories	62
Fat	2 g
Saturated	1.2 g
Monounsaturated	0.6 g
Polyunsaturated	0.1 g
Carbohydrates	10.3 g
Cholesterol	5.2 mg
Protein	1 g
Fiber	0.4 g
Calories from fat	29%

Ingredients

Dough

¼ cup butter or non-hydrogenated margarine, softened
⅓ cup sugar
⅓ cup packed brown sugar
1 large egg
2 tsp vanilla
1¼ cups flour
¼ tsp baking soda
¼ tsp salt

Filling

2 Tbsp liquid honey, maple syrup or corn syrup
2 Tbsp packed brown sugar
½ tsp cinnamon
2 Tbsp finely chopped walnuts or pecans

Nutrition Facts

Per cookie

Calories	55
Fat	1.7 g
Saturated	0.9 g
Monounsaturated	0.5 g
Polyunsaturated	0.2 g
Carbohydrates	9.2 g
Cholesterol	9.4 mg
Protein	0.7 g
Fiber	0.2 g
Calories from fat	28%

Cinnamon Bun Crunch Icebox Cookies

This is the crunchy cookie version of cinnamon buns, swirled with brown sugar and cinnamon. To make them look even more authentic, drizzle the cooled cookies with 1 cup icing sugar blended with 2 Tbsp milk and ½ tsp vanilla.

In a medium bowl, beat the butter, sugar and brown sugar with an electric mixer for a minute, until well combined. Add the egg and vanilla and beat until smooth. Add the flour, baking soda and salt and stir by hand just until you have a soft dough.

Roll the dough between two sheets of waxed or parchment paper into a 12-inch square. Place on a cookie sheet in the fridge for about 30 minutes or in the freezer for 15 minutes to firm it up a little.

Remove the dough from the fridge and peel off the top layer of waxed paper. Drizzle honey evenly over the square of dough, then sprinkle with brown sugar, cinnamon and nuts, going almost to the edges. Starting from a long edge, gently roll into a log, peeling back the paper as you go. Wrap in waxed paper or plastic wrap and freeze for 3 hours or up to 3 months.

When you're ready to bake, preheat the oven to 350°F. Slice the log into ¼ inch thick slices and place an inch apart on a cookie sheet sprayed with non-stick spray. Bake for 12–15 minutes, until pale golden. Let cool on the cookie sheet for a few minutes before transferring to a wire rack to cool completely.

Makes 3 dozen cookies.

CLOCKWISE FROM LEFT: Chocolate Peanut Butter
Ribbons p. 101; Marmalade Hazelnut Swirls p. 102;
Chocolate Gingerbread p. 178; Cornmeal Maple
Pecan Twists p. 66; Molasses Crinkles p. 58

Basic Biscotti

Chunky Peanut Butter Biscotti

Double Chocolate Hazelnut Biscotti

Dried Cherry, Almond & White Chocolate Biscotti

Brownie Biscotti

Hazelnut Cappuccino Biscotti

Pumpkin Power Biscotti

Banana Bread Biscotti

Biscotti

Ingredients

2 Tbsp butter or non-hydrogenated margarine, softened
¾ cup sugar
2 large eggs
1 tsp vanilla
2 cups all-purpose flour
2 tsp baking powder
¼ tsp salt

Nutrition Facts
Per biscotto

Calories	78
Fat	1.5 g
Saturated	0.7 g
Monounsaturated	0.4 g
Polyunsaturated	0.1 g
Carbohydrates	14.3 g
Cholesterol	20.5 mg
Protein	1.6 g
Fiber	0.3 g
Calories from fat	17%

Basic Biscotti

Biscotti became popular along with coffee houses, and many consider biscotti to be the only low-fat choice in a café full of buttery cookies, muffins and scones. Contrary to popular belief, all biscotti are not low in fat—in fact, some contain as much fat as shortbread! However, it's easy to create low-fat biscotti; because of their hard and dry texture, you don't have to worry about losing tenderness like you would with a regular cookie. This basic biscotti recipe can be customized with grated citrus zest or ginger, spices, flavored extracts, and additions such as dried fruit, candied ginger, nuts and chocolate.

Preheat the oven to 350°F.

In a large bowl, beat the butter, sugar, eggs and vanilla until smooth. Add the flour, baking powder and salt and stir until almost combined; add any additions you want and stir just until blended. If it seems dry, use your hands to complete the mixing as the dough comes together.

Turn the dough out onto a floured surface. Divide in half and shape each piece into an 8-inch long log. Place the logs 2–3 inches apart on a cookie sheet sprayed with non-stick spray, and flatten each into a rectangle that's about 3 inches wide.

Bake for 20–25 minutes, until firm and starting to crack on top. Transfer the logs to a wire rack to cool for a bit and reduce the oven temperature to 275°F.

When they're cool enough to handle (they tend to crumble when they're still hot), place the logs on a cutting board, trim the ends and cut each log diagonally into ½–¾-inch slices with a serrated knife. Place the slices upright on the cookie sheet, spacing them about ½ inch apart so that there's room for the air to circulate between them, and return to the oven for 30 minutes. If you like, turn the heat off and leave the biscotti inside the oven until it cools down to make them even harder.

Makes 2 dozen biscotti.

Oatmeal Chocolate Chip Biscotti

Grind ¾ cup oats in a food processor until it has the texture of coarse flour, and use it in place of ½ cup of the flour. Add ½ cup chocolate chips to the dough along with the flour mixture. Adds 1 g fat per biscotto.

Orange Chocolate Chip Biscotti

Add the grated zest of an orange to the egg mixture and ½ cup chocolate chips along with the flour. Adds 1 g fat per biscotto.

Cranberry Orange Biscotti

Add the grated zest of an orange to the butter-sugar mixture and ½ cup chopped dried cranberries to the dough along with the flour. Fat content remains the same.

Cantuccini (Almond Biscotti)

For traditional Italian almond biscotti, use almond extract instead of vanilla and add 1 cup slivered or sliced almonds to the dough along with the flour. Adds about 2.3 g fat per biscotto, but only the healthy kind.

Almond Chocolate Chunk Biscotti

Use almond extract instead of vanilla and add 1 cup of slivered or sliced almonds and ½ cup chopped chocolate to the dough along with the flour. Adds 3.4 g fat per biscotto.

Lemon White Chocolate Biscotti

Add the grated zest of a lemon to the butter-sugar mixture and ½ cup white chocolate chunks or chips to the dough along with the flour. Adds 2 g fat per biscotto.

(continued next page)

Fruit & Nut Biscotti

Add ½ cup chopped dried fruit (such as raisins, apricots, dates, cranberries or cherries) and ½ cup chopped nuts (such as walnuts, pecans or almonds) to the dough along with the flour. Adds 1.5 g fat per biscotto.

Apricot Ginger Biscotti

Add 2 tsp grated fresh ginger (or 1 tsp powdered ginger) to the butter-sugar mixture and ½ cup chopped dried apricots and ½ cup chopped candied ginger along with the flour. Fat content remains the same.

Lemon Poppy Seed Biscotti

Add the grated zest of 1 or 2 lemons to the butter-sugar mixture and ¼ cup poppy seeds along with the flour. Fat content remains the same.

Green Tea Biscotti

Add 1 Tbsp matcha green tea powder to the flour mixture and add ½ cup slivered almonds or currants too, if you like. Almonds will add 1.6 g fat per biscotto, but only the good kind.

Chunky Peanut Butter Biscotti

These can be made using all white flour if you prefer, but the whole wheat flour adds a nutty flavor and extra fiber to these crunchy biscotti. When shaping your biscotti log, lightly dampen your hands with water so that the dough won't stick to them.

Preheat the oven to 350°F.

In a medium bowl, combine the flour, whole wheat flour, baking powder, baking soda and salt; set aside. In a large bowl, beat the peanut butter, sugar, brown sugar, egg, egg whites and vanilla until smooth.

Add the flour mixture, peanuts and chocolate chips to the peanut butter mixture and stir by hand just until combined. Turn the dough out onto a lightly floured surface, divide in half and shape each piece into an 8-inch long log. Place the logs about 2 inches apart on a cookie sheet sprayed with non-stick spray and flatten each so that it's about 3 inches wide.

Bake for 25–30 minutes, until firm and starting to crack on top. Place on a wire rack to cool for a bit and reduce the oven temperature to 275°F.

When they're cool enough to handle (they tend to crumble when they're still hot), place the logs on a cutting board, trim the ends and cut each log diagonally into ½–¾-inch slices with a serrated knife. Place the slices upright on the cookie sheet, spacing them about ½ inch apart so that there's room for the air to circulate between them, and return to the oven for 30 minutes. If you like, turn off the heat and leave the biscotti inside the oven until it cools down to make them even harder.

Makes 2 dozen biscotti.

Ingredients

1 cup all-purpose flour
1 cup whole wheat flour
1 tsp baking powder
½ tsp baking soda
¼ tsp salt
½ cup light or all-natural
    peanut butter
½ cup sugar
½ cup packed brown sugar
1 large egg
2 large egg whites
2 tsp vanilla
½ cup chopped dry or honey-
    roasted peanuts
½ cup chocolate chips
    (optional)

Nutrition Facts
Per biscotto

Calories	118
Fat	3.7 g
Saturated	0.6 g
Monounsaturated	1.6 g
Polyunsaturated	1.2 g
Carbohydrates	18.7 g
Cholesterol	9 mg
Protein	3.5 g
Fiber	1.1 g
Calories from fat	27%

Ingredients

2 cups all-purpose flour
1 cup sugar
⅓ cup cocoa
1 tsp baking soda
½ tsp salt
2 large eggs
2 large egg whites
1 tsp vanilla
1 tsp instant coffee, dissolved
    in 1 tsp water
½ cup chocolate chips or good
    quality chocolate, chopped
½–1 cup hazelnuts

Nutrition Facts

Per biscotto

Calories	125
Fat	3.7 g
Saturated	1.2 g
Monounsaturated	1.8 g
Polyunsaturated	0.5 g
Carbohydrates	20.9 g
Cholesterol	18.3 mg
Protein	2.9 g
Fiber	1.5 g
Calories from fat	26%

Double Chocolate Hazelnut Biscotti

Make these with hazelnuts, almonds, pecans…all nuts get along well with chocolate.

Some people consider thinness to be the most important characteristic of good biscotti; if you chill or freeze your biscotti log after its first baking, it will be easier to slice nice and thin, if you like it that way.

Preheat the oven to 350°F.

Place the hazelnuts on a dry cookie sheet and toast for 7–10 minutes, until the skins pop open and the nuts are fragrant. Remove from the oven and place in a clean kitchen towel. Rub the nuts in the towel until most of the skins rub off. Set the nuts aside. (If you're using any other type of nut, just toast them and don't worry about rubbing off the skins.)

In a large bowl, combine the flour, sugar, cocoa, baking soda and salt. In a medium bowl, stir together the eggs, egg whites, vanilla and coffee. Add the egg mixture, chocolate chips and hazelnuts to the flour mixture and stir by hand just until combined.

Turn the dough out onto a lightly floured surface. With floured or dampened hands, shape the dough into two 8-inch long logs. Place the logs about 2 inches apart on a cookie sheet that has been sprayed with non-stick spray and flatten each into a rectangle that's about 3 inches wide.

Bake for 25–30 minutes, until firm and cracked on top. Transfer to a wire rack to cool for a bit and reduce the oven temperature to 275°F.

When they're cool enough to handle (they tend to crumble when they're still hot), place the logs on a cutting board, trim the ends and cut each log diagonally into ½–¾-inch slices with a serrated knife. Place the slices upright on the cookie sheet, spacing them about ½ inch apart so that there's room for the air to circulate between them, and return to the oven for 30 minutes. If you like, turn the heat off and leave the biscotti inside the oven until it cools down to make them even harder.

Makes 2 dozen biscotti.

Orange Chocolate Hazelnut Biscotti
Add the grated zest of an orange to the egg mixture. Fat content remains the same.

Chocolate Hazelnut & Ginger Biscotti
Add ¼ cup chopped crystallized ginger along with the chocolate chips and hazelnuts. Fat content remains the same.

Dried Cherry, Almond & White Chocolate Biscotti

Dried cherries, almonds and white chocolate make gorgeous biscotti. If you like big, long biscotti, shape the dough into one 6-inch wide rectangle instead of two. For extra almond flavor, substitute almond extract for some or all of the vanilla.

Preheat the oven to 350°F.

In a large bowl, beat the butter and sugar until well combined; it will have the consistency of wet sand. Add the eggs and vanilla and beat until smooth.

Add the flour, baking powder and salt and stir until almost combined; add the cherries, chocolate and almonds and stir just until blended. If the mixture seems dry, use your hands to mix it until the dough comes together.

Turn the dough out onto a lightly floured surface, divide in half and shape each piece into an 8-inch long log. Place the logs about 2 inches apart on a cookie sheet sprayed with non-stick spray and flatten each into a rectangle about 3 inches wide.

Bake for 30–35 minutes, until golden and cracked on top. Transfer the logs to a wire rack to cool for a bit and reduce the oven temperature to 275°F.

When they're cool enough to handle (they tend to crumble when they're still hot), place the logs on a cutting board, trim the ends and cut each log diagonally into ½–¾-inch slices with a serrated knife. Place the slices upright on the cookie sheet, spacing them about ½ inch apart so that there's room for the air to circulate between them, and return to the oven for 30 minutes. If you like, turn the heat off and leave the biscotti inside the oven until it cools down to make them even harder.

Makes 2 dozen biscotti.

Ingredients

2 Tbsp butter or non-hydrogenated margarine, softened
¾ cup sugar
2 large eggs
2 tsp vanilla
2 cups all-purpose flour
2 tsp baking powder
¼ tsp salt
½ cup dried cherries or
  cranberries
⅔ cup coarsely chopped white
  chocolate
⅓ cup coarsely chopped,
  sliced or slivered almonds

Nutrition Facts
Per biscotto

Calories	109
Fat	3.7 g
Saturated	1.6 g
Monounsaturated	1.5 g
Polyunsaturated	0.4 g
Carbohydrates	17.1 g
Cholesterol	20 mg
Protein	2.2 g
Fiber	0.8 g
Calories from fat	30%

Brownie Biscotti

These are my favorite cookie to dunk in cold or warmed milk. They remind me of brownies, but because they're hard and must be dunked between bites, I'm forced to take my time rather than scarfing down half the pan, a common occurrence when I make brownies.

Preheat the oven to 350°F.

In a large bowl, beat the butter, sugar, eggs and vanilla until smooth. In a medium bowl, stir together the flour, cocoa, baking powder and salt. Add to the egg mixture and stir until almost combined; add the chocolate chips and walnuts and stir just until blended.

On a cookie sheet sprayed with non-stick spray, shape the dough into a 10-inch long log. Flatten it with your hands until it's 3–4 inches wide.

Bake for 30–35 minutes, until firm and cracked on top. Transfer the log to a wire rack to cool for a bit and reduce the oven temperature to 275°F.

When the log is cool enough to handle (they tend to crumble when they're hot), transfer to a cutting board and cut diagonally into ½–¾-inch slices with a serrated knife. Place the slices upright on the cookie sheet, spacing them about ½ inch apart so that there's room for the air to circulate between them, and return to the oven for 30 minutes. If you like, turn the heat off and leave the biscotti inside the oven until it cools down to make them even harder.

Makes about 15 biscotti.

Ingredients

2 Tbsp butter or non-hydrogenated margarine, softened
¾ cup sugar
2 large eggs
2 tsp vanilla
1⅔ cups all-purpose flour
⅓ cup cocoa
2 tsp baking powder
¼ tsp salt
½ cup chocolate chips or white chocolate chunks
¼ cup chopped pecans or walnuts

Nutrition Facts
Per biscotto

Calories	173
Fat	5.8 g
Saturated	2.7 g
Monounsaturated	2.1 g
Polyunsaturated	0.8 g
Carbohydrates	27.6 g
Cholesterol	33.4 mg
Protein	3.3 g
Fiber	2 g
Calories from fat	30%

Ingredients

2½ cups all-purpose flour
1 cup sugar
½ tsp baking soda
½ tsp baking powder
½ tsp cinnamon (optional)
½ tsp salt
¼ cup strong coffee, cooled
1 Tbsp milk
2 large eggs
1 tsp vanilla
¾ cup hazelnuts, toasted
    and left whole or coarsely
    chopped
½ cup chocolate chips or
    chopped white chocolate

Nutrition Facts

Per biscotto

Calories	129
Fat	4 g
Saturated	1.1 g
Monounsaturated	2.2 g
Polyunsaturated	0.6 g
Carbohydrates	20.7 g
Cholesterol	17 mg
Protein	2.6 g
Fiber	1.1 g
Calories from fat	28%

Hazelnut Cappuccino Biscotti

Packed with hazelnuts and chocolate, these go very well with a cuppa Joe. For a glossy finish, try brushing the tops of the logs with an egg white beaten with 1 tsp water before you bake them. (This works well with any biscotti.)

Preheat the oven to 350°F.

In a large bowl, stir together the flour, sugar, baking soda, baking powder, cinnamon and salt. In a medium bowl whisk together the coffee, milk, eggs and vanilla. Add the coffee mixture to the flour mixture and stir by hand until almost combined; add the hazelnuts and chocolate chips and stir until you have a soft dough.

Turn the dough out onto a lightly floured surface. With floured or dampened hands, shape the dough into two 8-inch long logs. Place the logs about 2 inches apart on a cookie sheet sprayed with non-stick spray and flatten each into a rectangle that's about 3 inches wide.

Bake for 20–25 minutes, until golden and firm. Transfer the logs to a wire rack to cool for a bit and reduce the oven temperature to 275°F.

When they're cool enough to handle (they tend to crumble when they're still hot), place the logs on a cutting board, trim the ends and cut each log diagonally into ½–¾-inch slices with a serrated knife. Place the slices upright on the cookie sheet, spacing them about ½ inch apart so that there's room for the air to circulate between them, and return to the oven for 30 minutes. If you like, turn the heat off and leave the biscotti inside the oven until it cools down to make them even harder.

Makes 2 dozen biscotti.

ON THE MAT: Hazelnut Cappuccino Biscotti p. 118;
IN THE MUG: Brownie Biscotti p. 117; Dried Cherry,
Almond & White Chocolate Biscotti p. 116;
Hazelnut Cappuccino Biscotti p. 118

Ingredients

1 cup all-purpose flour
½ cup whole wheat flour
½ cup low fat soy flour
¼ cup ground flax seed
½ cup sugar or brown sugar
1 tsp baking powder
½ tsp cinnamon
¼ tsp salt
½ cup canned pure pumpkin
 or mashed ripe banana
2 Tbsp canola, olive or flax oil
1 large egg
2 tsp vanilla
½ cup chopped walnuts or
 pecans

Nutrition Facts

Per biscotto

Calories	144
Fat	5.8 g
Saturated	0.5 g
Monounsaturated	2 g
Polyunsaturated	3 g
Carbohydrates	19.5 g
Cholesterol	14.4 mg
Protein	4.8 g
Fiber	1.6 g
Calories from fat	35%

Pumpkin Power Biscotti

These are higher in protein, fiber and mono- and polyunsaturated fats than most biscotti. Adding soy flour (available at most health food stores) boosts soy protein in any baked goods — it contains 20 grams per cup — but can be replaced with more whole wheat flour if you like.

Preheat the oven to 350°F.

In a medium bowl, combine the flours, sugar, baking powder, cinnamon and salt; set aside.

In a large bowl, stir together the pumpkin, oil, egg and vanilla; add to the flour mixture along with the walnuts and stir just until combined. If the mixture seems dry, use your hands to mix until the dough comes together.

On a cookie sheet sprayed with non-stick spray, shape the dough into a 10-inch long log. Flatten it with your hands until it's 3–4 inches wide.

Bake for 30–35 minutes, until firm and cracked on top. Transfer the log to a wire rack to cool for a bit and reduce the oven temperature to 275°F.

When the log is cool enough to handle (they tend to crumble when they're hot), transfer to a cutting board and cut diagonally into ½–¾-inch slices with a serrated knife. Place the slices upright on the cookie sheet, spacing them about ½ inch apart so that there's room for the air to circulate between them, and return to the oven for 30 minutes. If you like, turn the heat off and leave the biscotti inside the oven until it cools down to make them even harder.

Makes about 15 biscotti.

Banana Bread Biscotti

If you have a stash of black bananas but are sick of banana bread, try making these instead. For an extra treat, dip the cooled biscotti in melted chocolate, or drizzle melted chocolate over them.

Preheat the oven to 350°F.

In a medium bowl, combine the flours, sugar, baking powder, cinnamon and salt; set aside.

In a large bowl, stir together the banana, oil, egg and vanilla, but don't worry about getting all the lumps of banana out. Add the flour mixture and walnuts to the banana mixture and stir just until combined. If the mixture seems dry, use your hands to mix until the dough comes together.

On a cookie sheet sprayed with non-stick spray, shape the dough into a 10-inch long log. Flatten it with your hands until it's 3–4 inches wide.

Bake for 30–35 minutes, until firm and cracked on top. Transfer the log to a wire rack to cool for a bit and reduce the oven temperature to 275°F.

When the log is cool enough to handle (they tend to crumble when they're hot), transfer to a cutting board and cut diagonally into ½–¾-inch slices with a serrated knife. Place the slices upright on the cookie sheet, spacing them about ½ inch apart so that there's room for the air to circulate between them, and return to the oven for 30 minutes. If you like, turn the heat off and leave the biscotti inside the oven until it cools down to make them even harder.

Makes about 15 biscotti.

Banana Chocolate Chip Biscotti
Add ½ cup chocolate or peanut butter chips along with the walnuts. Adds 1 g fat per biscotto.

Ingredients

1 cup all-purpose flour
¾ cup whole wheat flour
½ cup sugar or brown sugar
1 tsp baking powder
½ tsp cinnamon
¼ tsp salt
½ cup mashed ripe banana
   (about 1 banana)
1 Tbsp canola oil
1 large egg
2 tsp vanilla
½ cup chopped walnuts or
   pecans

Nutrition Facts
Per biscotto

Calories	134
Fat	3.9 g
Saturated	0.4 g
Monounsaturated	1.2 g
Polyunsaturated	2 g
Carbohydrates	20.4 g
Cholesterol	14.4 mg
Protein	3.5 g
Fiber	1.6 g
Calories from fat	26%

Butter Tart Squares

Old-Fashioned Raisin Squares

Classic Lemon Bars

Hello Dollies

Rocky Road Squares

Peanut Brittle Squares

Cranberry Coconut Squares

Pecan Pie Squares

Carrot Pumpkin Bars

Fruit & Nut Energy Bars

Lemon Meringue Squares with Pecans

Creamy Key Lime Squares

Blueberry Cheesecake Squares

Apple Crumble Bars

Date Squares

Double Berry Crumble Squares

Butterscotch Nut Meringue Squares

Chewy Chocolate Chip Bars

Banana Nut Bars

Chunky Apple Bars

Spiced Zucchini Bars with Cranberries & Pecans

Squares & Bars

Butter Tart Squares

Butter tarts are a Canadian creation, perfected of course by my grandma. These are far less finicky than those that require shaping pastry shells, and contain far less fat as well, but the oozy, gooey filling packed with plump raisins and crunchy pecans make them every bit as authentic.

Preheat the oven to 350°F.

In a medium bowl, stir together the butter and brown sugar until creamy. Add the flour and salt and stir until well combined and crumbly.

Press into the bottom of an 8- × 8-inch pan sprayed with non-stick spray. Bake for 8–10 minutes, until just barely golden around the edges.

Using the same bowl (no need to wash it), combine the brown sugar, flour, baking powder and salt. Add the eggs and vanilla and stir until well blended and smooth. Stir in the raisins and pecans.

Pour over the base and return to the oven for 25–30 minutes, until golden and bubbly around the edges, but still slightly jiggly in the middle. The topping will puff up a bit as it bakes and then settle again when you remove it from the oven. Cool completely in the pan on a wire rack.

Makes 16 squares.

Ingredients

Base

¼ cup butter, softened
¼ cup packed brown sugar
1 cup all-purpose flour
pinch salt

Topping

1½ cups packed brown sugar
1 Tbsp all-purpose flour
¼ tsp baking powder
pinch salt
2 large eggs
1 tsp vanilla
¾ cup raisins
⅓ cup chopped pecans

Nutrition Facts

Per square

Calories	194
Fat	5.1 g
Saturated	2.1 g
Monounsaturated	2 g
Polyunsaturated	0.6 g
Carbohydrates	36.2 g
Cholesterol	34.7 mg
Protein	2.2 g
Fiber	1 g
Calories from fat	23%

Old-Fashioned Raisin Squares

These are similar to Butter Tart Squares but have an oatmeal base, no nuts and even more raisins. They remind me of my great aunt's raisin pie. The nutritional benefits of grapes are concentrated into raisins, making them rich in fiber, iron, selenium, potassium and B vitamins. They help to reduce cholesterol and high blood pressure and especially benefit those suffering from fatigue, depression or anxiety. And they taste good too.

Preheat the oven to 350°F.

In a medium bowl, stir together the butter and brown sugar until creamy. Add flour, oats, baking powder and salt, and mix until well combined and crumbly.

Press into the bottom of an 8- × 8-inch pan sprayed with non-stick spray. Bake for 8–10 minutes, until just barely golden around the edges.

In the same bowl (no need to wash it) stir together the brown sugar and flour. Add the eggs and vanilla and stir until well blended and smooth. Stir in the raisins and pour over the base.

Bake for 25–30 minutes, until golden and set around the edges but still just slightly jiggly in the middle. Cool completely in the pan on a wire rack before cutting into squares.

Makes 16 squares.

Ingredients

Base
¼ cup butter, softened
¼ cup packed brown sugar
½ cup all-purpose flour
¾ cup oats
¼ tsp baking powder
pinch salt

Topping
1½ cups packed brown sugar
1 Tbsp all-purpose flour
2 large eggs
1 tsp vanilla
1–1½ cups raisins

Nutrition Facts
Per square

Calories	191
Fat	3.9 g
Saturated	2.1 g
Monounsaturated	1.2 g
Polyunsaturated	0.3 g
Carbohydrates	38.2 g
Cholesterol	34.7 mg
Protein	2.3 g
Fiber	1.3 g
Calories from fat	18%

Classic Lemon Bars

I haven't yet met anyone who doesn't love lemon bars and many who would choose them over chocolate. These are classic lemon bars with a shortbread base, but this version uses half the fat of a traditional shortbread crust. It will seem crumbly and dry as you press it into the pan, but trust me, it works!

Preheat the oven to 350°F.

In a medium bowl, stir together the butter and sugar until creamy. Add the flour and salt and stir until well combined and crumbly.

Press into the bottom of an 8- × 8-inch pan sprayed with non-stick spray. Bake for 8–10 minutes, until just barely golden around the edges.

In the same bowl (no need to wash it), stir together the sugar, flour, baking powder and salt. Add the egg, egg white, lemon zest and juice and stir until well blended and smooth. Pour over the base.

Return to the oven for 25–30 minutes, until slightly golden on top and bubbly around the edges. Cool completely in the pan on a wire rack. Sprinkle with icing sugar before cutting into bars.

Makes 12 bars.

Hazelnut or Almond Lemon Bars
Stir ½ cup flaked hazelnuts or sliced almonds into the base mixture and bake as directed. Sprinkle another ¼ cup nuts over the lemon mixture before the second baking. Adds 1.7 g fat per bar, but only the healthy kind.

Raspberry or Apricot Lemon Bars
After baking the crust, spread with about ¼ cup raspberry or apricot jam. Pour lemon topping over the jam and bake as directed. Fat content remains the same.

Ingredients

Base
¼ cup butter, softened
¼ cup sugar
1 scant cup all-purpose flour
pinch salt
Topping
1 cup sugar
2 Tbsp all-purpose flour
¼ tsp baking powder
pinch salt
1 large egg
1 large egg white
grated zest of 1 lemon
juice of 1 lemon (3 Tbsp)
icing sugar, for sprinkling

Nutrition Facts
Per bar

Calories	168
Fat	4.4 g
Saturated	2.5 g
Monounsaturated	1.3 g
Polyunsaturated	0.2 g
Carbohydrates	30.8 g
Cholesterol	28.3 mg
Protein	2.1 g
Fiber	0.4 g
Calories from fat	23%

CLOCKWISE FROM LEFT: Chewy Chocolate Chip Bars p. 142; Chunky Peanut Crunch Cookies (without the cherries) p. 63; Classic Lemon Bars p. 126

Ingredients

Base

1¼ cups graham crumbs

¼ cup sugar

2 Tbsp butter or non-hydrogenated margarine, melted

1 Tbsp corn syrup or liquid
honey

Topping

½ cup shredded coconut,
sweetened or unsweetened

½ cup chocolate chips

1 cup chopped walnuts or
pecans

1 can sweetened condensed
milk

Nutrition Facts

Per square

Calories	220
Fat	10.9 g
Saturated	4.2 g
Monounsaturated	2.7 g
Polyunsaturated	3.6 g
Carbohydrates	27.5 g
Cholesterol	11 mg
Protein	4.5 g
Fiber	1.2 g
Calories from fat	43%

Hello Dollies

This slimmed-down version of Hello Dollies (also known as Magic Bars) contain almost half the fat of those made with a traditional recipe. Because there's no substitute for rich, gooey layers of chocolate, coconut and nuts, I reduced the fat in the base and adjusted the proportions of each ingredient to keep the saturated fat as low as possible.

Preheat the oven to 325°F.

In a medium bowl, combine the graham crumbs, sugar, butter and corn syrup and stir until well blended. Press into the bottom of an 8- × 8-inch pan sprayed with non-stick spray.

Sprinkle with coconut, chocolate chips and nuts. Pour the sweetened condensed milk evenly over top.

Bake for 30–35 minutes, until golden (they'll be just barely golden in the middle) and bubbly around the edges. Cool completely in the pan on a wire rack.

Makes 16 squares.

Rocky Road Squares

These fast and easy squares have a brown sugar and whole wheat shortbread base covered with a jumble of creamy caramel, crunchy nuts, gooey chocolate and toasted marshmallows.

Preheat the oven to 350°F.

In a medium bowl, stir together the butter and brown sugar until creamy. Add the flour and salt and stir until well combined and crumbly.

Press into the bottom of an 8- × 8-inch pan sprayed with non-stick spray. Bake for 8–10 minutes, until just barely golden around the edges.

Spread the butterscotch topping over the crust. Sprinkle with marshmallows, nuts and chocolate chips. Bake for another 10 minutes, until the marshmallows are puffy and golden. Cool in the pan on a wire rack before cutting into squares.

Makes 16 squares.

Salted Peanut Squares

Substitute salted peanuts for the walnuts, and peanut butter chips for the chocolate chips. Fat content remains the same.

Ingredients

Base
¼ cup butter, softened
¼ cup packed brown sugar
1 scant cup whole wheat flour
pinch salt

Topping
½ cup caramel or butterscotch ice cream topping (such as Hershey's Top Scotch)
1½ cups mini marshmallows
⅓ cup chopped walnuts or pecans
¼ cup chocolate chips, chopped if you like

Nutrition Facts
Per square

Calories	150
Fat	5.8 g
Saturated	2.7 g
Monounsaturated	1.5 g
Polyunsaturated	1.3 g
Carbohydrates	23.8 g
Cholesterol	8.2 mg
Protein	2.3 g
Fiber	1.4 g
Calories from fat	33%

Ingredients

Base
¼ cup butter, softened
¼ cup packed brown sugar
1 cup all-purpose flour
pinch salt

Topping
1 cup salted peanuts
⅔ cup caramel or butterscotch
    topping (such as Hershey's
    Top Scotch)
2 Tbsp all-purpose flour

Nutrition Facts
Per square

Calories	158
Fat	7.5 g
Saturated	2.4 g
Monounsaturated	3.1 g
Polyunsaturated	1.6 g
Carbohydrates	21 g
Cholesterol	8 mg
Protein	3.3 g
Fiber	1.1 g
Calories from fat	40%

Peanut Brittle Squares

Although these are higher in fat than other cookies in this book, most of the fat comes from the peanuts. Peanuts are known to lower LDL (bad) cholesterol, raise HDL (good) cholesterol, and contain antioxidants, folic acid, fiber and resveratrol, the same cancer-preventing, heart-healthy antioxidant found in red wine.

Preheat the oven to 350°F.

In a medium bowl, stir together the butter and brown sugar until creamy. Add the flour and salt and stir until well combined and crumbly.

Press into the bottom of an 8- × 8-inch pan sprayed with non-stick spray. Bake for 8–10 minutes, until just barely golden around the edges.

Spread the peanuts over the base. Using the same bowl (no need to wash it), mix the butterscotch topping and flour until smooth. Pour evenly over the peanuts.

Bake for 20 minutes, until the topping is golden and bubbly. Cool completely in the pan on a wire rack.

Makes 16 squares.

Cranberry Coconut Squares

The berries and coconut in these squares are held together by a lemon filling that creates a deliciously crunchy top as it bakes. If you want to slice them nice and cleanly, freeze them first—also a good idea if you're making them ahead of time for a party. Cut the frozen squares and put them out on a plate; by the time it's time to eat they'll have thawed nicely.

Preheat the oven to 350°F.

In a medium bowl, stir together the butter and sugar until creamy. Add the flour and salt and stir until well combined and crumbly.

Press into the bottom of an 8- × 8-inch pan sprayed with non-stick spray. Bake for 8–10 minutes, until just barely golden around the edges.

In the same bowl (no need to wash it), combine the sugar, flour, baking powder and salt. Add the egg, egg white and lemon juice and stir until well blended and smooth.

Sprinkle cranberries and coconut evenly over the base, and pour the lemon filling over top. Bake for 40 minutes, until golden and set. Cool completely in the pan on a wire rack. Sprinkle with icing sugar before cutting into squares.

Makes 16 squares.

Cranberry Coconut Squares with Almonds

Sprinkle ⅓ cup sliced almonds over the top before baking. Adds 1.5 g fat per square.

Ingredients

Base
¼ cup butter, softened
¼ cup sugar
1 scant cup all-purpose flour
pinch salt

Topping
1 cup sugar
2 Tbsp all-purpose flour
½ tsp baking powder
pinch salt
1 large egg
1 large egg white
¼ cup lemon juice
1½ cups fresh or frozen
    cranberries, blueberries or
    raspberries
½ cup shredded coconut
icing sugar for sprinkling

Nutrition Facts
Per square

Calories	130
Fat	3.3 g
Saturated	1.9 g
Monounsaturated	1 g
Polyunsaturated	0.2 g
Carbohydrates	24 g
Cholesterol	21 mg
Protein	1.6 g
Fiber	0.7 g
Calories from fat	23%

Pecan Pie Squares

Pecan pie is one of the richest, highest-in-fat desserts you can eat. It's also one of the best. I recently came across a recipe for pecan pie bars that contained 74 grams of fat each! These contain less than 8 grams, most of which comes from the pecans, which means healthy mono- and polyunsaturated fats.

Preheat the oven to 375°F.

In a medium bowl, stir together the butter and brown sugar until creamy. Add the flour and salt and stir until well combined and crumbly.

Press into the bottom of an 8- × 8-inch pan sprayed with non-stick spray. Bake for 8–10 minutes, until just barely golden around the edges.

In the same bowl (no need to wash it), stir together the brown sugar and flour. (Stirring the flour and sugar together first gets rid of any lumps in the flour.) Add the eggs, corn syrup, vanilla and salt and mix until smooth.

Arrange the pecans evenly over the crust and pour the filling over top. Bake for 25–30 minutes, until puffed and golden. Cool in the pan on a wire rack.

Makes 16 squares.

Chocolate Chunk Pecan Pie Squares
Sprinkle ½ cup chocolate chips or chunks over the pecans. Bake as directed. Adds 1.6 g fat per square.

Cranberry Pecan Pie Squares
Sprinkle ½ cup coarsely chopped fresh, frozen or dried cranberries over the pecans. Bake as directed. Fat content remains the same.

Ingredients

Base
¼ cup butter, softened
¼ cup packed brown sugar
1 cup all-purpose flour
pinch salt

Filling
½ cup packed brown sugar
1 Tbsp all-purpose flour
2 large eggs
¾ cup corn syrup or liquid
   honey
1 tsp vanilla
¼ tsp salt
1 cup pecan halves

Nutrition Facts
Per square

Calories	194
Fat	8.2 g
Saturated	2.4 g
Monounsaturated	3.9 g
Polyunsaturated	1.4 g
Carbohydrates	29.3 g
Cholesterol	34.7 mg
Protein	2.2 g
Fiber	0.7 g
Calories from fat	36%

Carrot Pumpkin Bars

Carrot and pumpkin deliver a double whammy of vitamin A in the form of beta carotene; to boost it even more, add a big spoonful of tomato paste (after all, tomatoes are fruit) to the pumpkin mixture. These are fab spread with the Lemon Cream Cheese Frosting on page 198.

Preheat the oven to 350°F.

In a medium bowl, combine the flour, baking powder, baking soda, cinnamon and salt; set aside. In a large bowl, beat the egg and egg white until foamy. Beat in the brown sugar, pumpkin, oil, orange zest and vanilla until smooth.

Add the flour mixture to the egg mixture and stir by hand until almost combined; add the carrots, raisins, cranberries and nuts and stir just until blended.

Spread the batter into an 8- × 8-inch pan sprayed with non-stick spray. Bake for 30–35 minutes, until the top is springy to the touch. Cool in the pan on a wire rack.

Makes 12 bars.

Ingredients

1 cup all-purpose flour
1 tsp baking powder
¼ tsp baking soda
½ tsp cinnamon
¼ tsp salt
1 large egg
1 large egg white
1 cup packed brown sugar
½ cup canned pumpkin
¼ cup canola oil
grated zest of 1 orange
1 tsp vanilla
½ cup packed grated carrots
   (about 1 large carrot)
½ cup raisins
⅓ cup dried cranberries or
   chopped dried apricots
⅓ cup chopped walnuts or
   pecans

Nutrition Facts
Per bar

Calories	212
Fat	7 g
Saturated	0.6 g
Monounsaturated	3.3 g
Polyunsaturated	2.8 g
Carbohydrates	35.3 g
Cholesterol	18 mg
Protein	3.3 g
Fiber	1.9 g
Calories from fat	29%

Ingredients

4 packed cups dried fruit
(such as raisins, figs,
apricots, cranberries, dates,
cherries, apples, peaches
and prunes)
1 cup orange or grape juice
1 cup chopped walnuts, pecans, hazelnuts or almonds
2 large eggs
1 cup packed brown sugar
½ cup all-purpose flour
½ cup whole wheat flour
½ tsp baking powder
¼ tsp salt

Nutrition Facts

Per bar

Calories	151
Fat	3.3 g
Saturated	0.3 g
Monounsaturated	0.8 g
Polyunsaturated	1.9 g
Carbohydrates	30 g
Cholesterol	16.6 mg
Protein	3 g
Fiber	2.5 g
Calories from fat	18%

Fruit & Nut Energy Bars

These bars travel well, making them perfect to pack along on a hike or any activity you need a healthy burst of energy for. The small amount of batter, which you can flavor with a sprinkle of cinnamon or the grated zest of an orange or lemon, is just enough to bind together any assortment of dried fruits and nuts you choose.

Chop the dried fruit so that it's roughly the same size as the raisins (you don't need to chop the raisins). Place in a sealed container or bowl along with the juice, stir it up and let it stand for an hour or overnight, stirring or shaking the container once in a while. It should absorb all the juice.

When ready to mix and bake, preheat the oven to 350°F.

In a large bowl, beat the eggs and egg white for 1 minute, until foamy. Add the sugar and beat for another minute, until thickened.

In a small bowl, combine the flour, whole wheat flour, baking powder and salt. Add to the egg mixture and stir by hand just until combined. Gently stir in the fruit mixture (along with any juice that hasn't been absorbed) and the nuts.

Spread the batter into a 9- × 13-inch pan sprayed with non-stick spray. Bake for 25–30 minutes, until golden and springy to the touch. Cool in the pan on a wire rack.

Makes 20 bars.

Trail Mix Bars

Substitute 1 cup chocolate chips for 1 cup of the dried fruit, and use peanuts instead of walnuts. Bake as directed. Adds 2.5 g fat per bar.

Lemon Meringue Squares with Pecans

I started making these instead of lemon meringue pie, which everyone loves but requires a time commitment I can't always make. I snuck some pecans into the base and meringue for extra flavor and healthy fats; if you like, leave them out and bump the flour in the base to 1 cup.

Preheat the oven to 350°F.

In the bowl of a food processor, pulse all the base ingredients until well blended. Alternatively, beat the butter and sugar in a medium bowl until creamy; add the flour, pecans and salt and stir until well combined and crumbly.

Press into the bottom of an 8- × 8-inch pan that has been sprayed with non-stick spray. Bake for about 10 minutes, until barely golden around the edges. In the same bowl (no need to wash it), stir together the sugar and flour. Add the eggs, lemon zest and juice and stir until well blended and smooth. Pour over the base and return to the oven for 20–25 minutes, until topping is set and no longer appears wet. Remove from the oven and increase the heat to 400°F.

In a clean glass or stainless steel bowl, beat the egg whites until soft peaks form. Gradually add the sugar and continue beating until the meringue is stiff and glossy. Gently fold in the pecans. Spread over the lemon filling and return to the oven for 7–10 minutes, until golden. Cool in the pan on a wire rack.

Makes 16 squares.

Lime Meringue & Pecan Bars

Replace the lemon zest with the zest of 2 limes, and the lemon juice with lime juice. Fat content remains the same.

Ingredients

Base
¼ cup butter, softened
¼ cup sugar
¾ cup flour
¼ cup finely chopped pecans
pinch salt
Topping
1 cup sugar
¼ cup all-purpose flour
2 large eggs
grated zest of 1 lemon
½ cup lemon juice
Meringue
2 large egg whites
⅓ cup sugar
¼ cup finely chopped pecans

Nutrition Facts
Per square

Calories	166
Fat	5.9 g
Saturated	2.2 g
Monounsaturated	2.5 g
Polyunsaturated	0.8 g
Carbohydrates	27 g
Cholesterol	34.7 mg
Protein	2.3 g
Fiber	0.5 g
Calories from fat	31%

Ingredients

Base

¼ cup butter, softened
¼ cup sugar
1 scant cup all-purpose flour
pinch salt

Filling

3 Tbsp sugar
2 Tbsp cornstarch
1 can sweetened condensed milk
1 large egg
grated zest of 2 limes
½ cup lime juice

Nutrition Facts

Per square

Calories	147
Fat	4.9 g
Saturated	3 g
Monounsaturated	1.4 g
Polyunsaturated	0.3 g
Carbohydrates	23.3 g
Cholesterol	27.7 mg
Protein	2.8 g
Fiber	0.3 g
Calories from fat	30%

Creamy Key Lime Squares

These have a consistency similar to cheesecake. Because real key limes are often hard to find, you can use the regular gin & tonic limes that are always available at the supermarket. (The key lime is a specific variety of lime with a distinctive flavor and aroma; they're much smaller and rounder in size, with a thin, smooth and greenish-yellow peel. The interior is also greenish-yellow, quite juicy and has a higher acidity than regular limes.)

Preheat the oven to 350°F.

In a medium bowl, stir together the butter and sugar until creamy. Add the flour and salt and stir until well combined and crumbly.

Press into the bottom of an 8- × 8-inch pan sprayed with non-stick spray. Bake for 8–10 minutes, until just barely golden around the edges.

In a medium bowl, combine the sugar and cornstarch. Stir in the sweetened condensed milk, egg, lime zest and juice until smooth. Pour over the crust.

Bake for 25–30 minutes, until the edges are set but the center is still slightly jiggly. Let cool in the pan on a wire rack. When cool, cover and refrigerate until well chilled. Store leftovers tightly covered in the refrigerator.

Makes 16 squares.

Blueberry Cheesecake Squares

These also have the texture of cheesecake, with about a third of the fat and calories. As an added benefit you won't end up with an entire cheesecake in your fridge, begging you to eat it.

Preheat the oven to 325°F.

In a medium bowl, combine the graham crumbs, sugar, butter and corn syrup and stir until well blended. Press into the bottom of an 8- × 8-inch pan sprayed with non-stick spray. Bake for 10–12 minutes, until pale golden around the edges.

In a medium bowl, beat the cream cheese until creamy and smooth. Add the icing sugar, egg, lemon juice and zest and beat on high speed for a minute or two, until thickened and smooth.

Pour the topping over the crust and sprinkle with blueberries. (Alternately, you can gently stir the berries into the cheesecake topping before spreading over the crust.)

Bake for 30–35 minutes, until the topping is slightly golden around the edges and no longer appears wet. Don't worry about the area around the berries appearing juicy. Cool in the pan on a wire rack, then refrigerate until well chilled. Store extras tightly covered in the refrigerator.

Makes 16 squares.

Ingredients

Base
1¼ cups graham crumbs
¼ cup sugar
2 Tbsp butter or non-hydrogenated margarine, melted
1 Tbsp corn syrup or liquid honey

Topping
one 8-oz pkg light cream cheese, softened
¾ cup icing sugar
1 large egg
2 Tbsp lemon juice
grated zest of 1 lemon (optional)
1½ cups fresh or frozen blueberries

Nutrition Facts
Per square

Calories	123
Fat	5.2 g
Saturated	2.7 g
Monounsaturated	1.7 g
Polyunsaturated	0.4 g
Carbohydrates	17.4 g
Cholesterol	26.3 mg
Protein	2.3 g
Fiber	0.5 g
Calories from fat	37%

Ingredients

Base

¼ cup butter, softened
¼ cup packed brown sugar
1 cup all-purpose flour
pinch salt

Topping

4–5 tart apples (such as
    Granny Smith)
⅓ cup raisins or dried
    cranberries (optional)
¼ cup packed brown sugar
¼ tsp cinnamon
2 tsp cornstarch
1 Tbsp lemon juice

Crumble

⅓ cup all-purpose flour
⅓ cup oats
¼ cup packed brown sugar
2 Tbsp butter or non-hydroge-
    nated margarine, melted

Nutrition Facts

Per bar

Calories	213
Fat	6.3 g
Saturated	3.7 g
Monounsaturated	1.7 g
Polyunsaturated	0.4 g
Carbohydrates	38.5 g
Cholesterol	15.5 mg
Protein	2.1 g
Fiber	1.9 g
Calories from fat	26%

Apple Crumble Bars

These are halfway between apple pie and apple crumble: both are the epitome of comfort desserts, but both require a fork. These you can carry around and eat with your fingers, or top with a scoop of light vanilla ice cream while still warm, and eat out of a bowl with a spoon.

Preheat the oven to 350°F.

In a medium bowl, stir together the butter and brown sugar until creamy. Add the flour and salt and stir until well combined and crumbly.

Press into the bottom of an 8- × 8-inch pan sprayed with non-stick spray. Bake for 8–10 minutes, until just barely golden around the edges.

Peel, core and coarsely dice the apples. You should end up with 4–5 cups.

In a large skillet, combine the apples, raisins, brown sugar and cinnamon. Cook over medium heat, stirring occasionally, for 5–7 minutes, until the apples are tender but still firm. In a small cup, stir together the cornstarch and lemon juice. Add to the apple mixture and cook, stirring constantly for 3 minutes, until thickened. Spoon evenly over the base.

In a medium bowl, blend together the flour, oats, brown sugar and butter with a fork or your fingers until well combined and crumbly. Sprinkle over the apple mixture. Bake for 25–30 minutes, until golden. Cool in the pan on a wire rack.

Makes 12 bars.

Date Squares

Date squares, also affectionately known as matrimonial slice for their popularity at weddings and showers, are popular for their nostalgic quality as well as nutritional value: dates and oats are both Good Things, and it's easy to slip a spoonful of ground flaxseed into either mixture as well. It's also easy to make substitutions for the date filling—try using all-fruit mincemeat instead.

Preheat the oven to 350°F.

In a large bowl, combine the flour, oats, brown sugar, baking soda and salt. Add the butter and stir until the mixture is well combined and crumbly. Press half the crumbs into an 8- × 8-inch pan sprayed with non-stick spray.

Combine the dates, brown sugar and water in a small saucepan over medium heat. Bring to a simmer and cook, stirring often, for 5–10 minutes or until thick and jam-like. Remove from the heat and stir in the lemon juice.

Spread the filling over the crust, and sprinkle with the remaining crumbs. Bake for 30–35 minutes, until golden around the edges. Cool in the pan on a wire rack.

Makes 16 squares.

Orange Rhubarb Squares

Combine 3 cups chopped rhubarb, 1½ cups sugar, 2 Tbsp cornstarch and the grated zest of an orange in a medium saucepan. Cook over medium heat, stirring often, for about 10 minutes or until thick. Use in place of the date filling. Fat content remains the same.

Ingredients

Base & Topping
1 cup all-purpose or whole
   wheat flour, or a combination
1 cup oats
⅔ cup packed brown sugar
¼ tsp baking soda
¼ tsp salt
⅓ cup butter, melted

Date Filling
½ lb (250 g) pitted dates,
   chopped (about 2 cups)
⅓ cup packed brown sugar
1 cup water or orange juice
1 Tbsp lemon juice

Nutrition Facts
Per square

Calories	195
Fat	4.7 g
Saturated	2.5 g
Monounsaturated	1.3 g
Polyunsaturated	0.4 g
Carbohydrates	37.4 g
Cholesterol	10.4 mg
Protein	2.8 g
Fiber	1.6 g
Calories from fat	21%

Double Berry Crumble Squares

Like berry crisp, these make a perfect summertime dessert served warm with a scoop of ice cream. To reduce the fat even further, use only ¼ cup melted butter and 1–2 Tbsp of juice in the crumble mixture. Boost the fiber even further by using half or all whole wheat flour and/or adding a sprinkle of ground flaxseed.

Preheat the oven to 350°F.

In a large bowl, combine the flour, oats, brown sugar, baking soda and salt, breaking up any lumps of brown sugar. Add the melted butter and mix, blending with your fingertips if necessary until you have a crumbly mixture. Remove 1 cup and set aside.

Press the remaining crumbs evenly into an 8- × 8-inch pan sprayed with non-stick spray. In a medium bowl stir together the berries, jam and flour; spread evenly over the base. Sprinkle reserved crumbs over top.

Bake for 30–35 minutes, until bubbly around the edges. Cool in the pan on a wire rack.

Makes 16 squares.

Cranberry-Orange Crumble Squares

Use fresh or frozen cranberries and orange marmalade in place of the berries and jam. Fat content remains the same.

Ingredients

Base & Topping
1 cup all-purpose flour
1 cup oats
½ cup packed brown sugar
¼ tsp baking soda
¼ tsp salt
⅓ cup butter or non-hydroge-nated margarine, melted

Filling
2 cups fresh or frozen (unthawed) blueberries, raspberries, halved straw-berries, blackberries or a combination
½ cup raspberry or other berry jam
2 tsp all-purpose flour

Nutrition Facts

Per square

Calories	148
Fat	4.4 g
Saturated	2.5 g
Monounsaturated	1.3 g
Polyunsaturated	0.3 g
Carbohydrates	26 g
Cholesterol	10.4 mg
Protein	1.9 g
Fiber	1.5 g
Calories from fat	26%

Butterscotch Nut Meringue Squares

The nuts sink into the middle, leaving them sandwiched between a rich, chewy butterscotch base and a light, crunchy meringue topping.

Preheat the oven to 350°F.

In a small saucepan, combine the butter and brown sugar over medium heat. Stir frequently until the edges bubble and the sugar dissolves, but don't bring it to a boil. Remove from the heat and transfer to a medium bowl to cool.

When the mixture has cooled to lukewarm, beat in the egg white and vanilla until smooth. Add the flour and salt, and stir by hand just until combined. Spread the batter into an 8- × 8-inch pan sprayed with non-stick spray.

In a clean glass or stainless steel bowl, beat the egg whites and salt until it holds soft peaks. Gradually add the sugar, beating until the mixture is stiff and glossy. Fold in the nuts and drop in spoonfuls over the butterscotch layer, then gently spread to cover.

Bake for 30–35 minutes, until the topping is puffy and golden. Cool completely in the pan on a wire rack.

Makes 16 squares.

Ingredients

Base
3 Tbsp butter
1 cup packed brown sugar
1 large egg white
1 tsp vanilla
½ cup all-purpose flour
¼ tsp salt

Topping
2 large egg whites
pinch salt
⅓ cup sugar
½ cup chopped walnuts or
  pecans

Nutrition Facts

Per square

Calories	137
Fat	4.4 g
Saturated	1.5 g
Monounsaturated	1.1 g
Polyunsaturated	1.6 g
Carbohydrates	23.2 g
Cholesterol	5.8 mg
Protein	2 g
Fiber	0.3 g
Calories from fat	28%

Chewy Chocolate Chip Bars

The ultimate quickie…when you need chocolate chip cookies fast.

Preheat the oven to 350°F.

In a medium bowl, stir together the butter and brown sugar. Add the egg and vanilla and stir until smooth. Add the flour, baking powder and salt and stir until almost combined; add the chocolate chips and stir just until blended.

Spread the batter into an 8- × 8-inch pan sprayed with non-stick spray; it will be fairly thin. Bake for 18–20 minutes, until pale golden around the edges. Don't overbake if you want them to be soft and chewy.

Makes 12 bars.

Chocolate Caramel Marshmallow Bars

Melt 20 caramels with 1 Tbsp milk in a small saucepan or on medium power in the microwave until smooth. When the bars come out of the oven, drizzle with the caramel mixture and sprinkle evenly with 1½ cups mini marshmallows. Return to the oven for 5–8 minutes, until the marshmallows are slightly puffed and golden. Cool in the pan on a wire rack. Adds 1 g fat.

Ingredients

2 Tbsp butter or non-hydrogenated margarine, softened
¾ cup packed brown sugar
1 large egg
1 tsp vanilla
¾ cup all-purpose flour
½ tsp baking powder
¼ tsp salt
½ cup chocolate chips

Nutrition Facts
Per bar

Calories	158
Fat	5.1 g
Saturated	3 g
Monounsaturated	1.4 g
Polyunsaturated	0.5 g
Carbohydrates	26 g
Cholesterol	23.8 mg
Protein	2 g
Fiber	1 g
Calories from fat	29%

Banana Nut Bars

These are quite moist and cakey in texture, almost like a snack cake. You can use all-purpose instead of whole wheat flour if you like. They're great with chocolate chips or topped with chocolate or Peanut Butter Frosting (see page 199).

Preheat the oven to 350°F.

In a large bowl, beat the butter, oil, sugar, brown sugar, egg and vanilla until smooth. Add bananas and stir until well blended. Don't worry about getting all the lumps out.

In a medium bowl, combine the flour, whole wheat flour, flaxseed, baking powder, baking soda, cinnamon and salt. Add to the banana mixture along with the nuts and stir by hand just until combined. The batter will be quite runny. Pour into an 8- × 8-inch pan sprayed with non-stick spray and bake for 35–40 minutes, until dark golden and the top is springy to the touch. Cool in the pan on a wire rack.

Makes 12 bars.

Chocolate Chip Banana Bars

Omit the cinnamon and add ½ cup chocolate chips along with the nuts. Bake as directed. Adds 2 g fat per bar.

Ingredients

2 Tbsp butter or non-hydrogenated margarine
2 Tbsp canola oil
½ cup sugar
½ cup packed brown sugar
1 large egg
1 tsp vanilla
1 cup mashed ripe banana
(about 2 bananas)
½ cup all-purpose flour
½ cup whole wheat flour
2 Tbsp ground flaxseed
(optional)
1 tsp baking powder
½ tsp baking soda
½ tsp cinnamon
¼ tsp salt
¼ cup chopped walnuts or
pecans

Nutrition Facts
Per bar

Calories	182
Fat	6.3 g
Saturated	1.6 g
Monounsaturated	2.4 g
Polyunsaturated	2 g
Carbohydrates	29.8 g
Cholesterol	23 mg
Protein	2.9 g
Fiber	1.2 g
Calories from fat	30%

Ingredients

1 large egg
1 large egg white
½ cup sugar
½ cup packed brown sugar
2 Tbsp butter or non-hydroge-
    nated margarine, melted
2 Tbsp canola oil
¼ cup applesauce
1 tsp vanilla
¾ cup all-purpose flour
¾ cup whole wheat flour
½ tsp baking powder
½ tsp cinnamon
¼ tsp salt
1 large apple, coarsely
    chopped (peeled or not)
Maple or Brown Sugar
    Frosting (optional, see
    pages 199 and 201)

Nutrition Facts

Per bar

Calories	184
Fat	4.9 g
Saturated	1.5 g
Monounsaturated	2.1 g
Polyunsaturated	1 g
Carbohydrates	33.5 g
Cholesterol	23 mg
Protein	2.7 g
Fiber	1.7 g
Calories from fat	23%

Chunky Apple Bars

More like a snack cake than a cookie, these are perfect for the fall, when apples are flavorful and abundant.

Preheat the oven to 350°F.

In a large bowl, combine the egg, egg white, sugar, brown sugar, butter, oil, applesauce and vanilla and stir until smooth.

In a medium bowl, combine the flour, baking powder, cinnamon and salt. Add to the egg mixture, and stir by hand until almost combined. Add apples and stir just until blended.

Spread the batter into an 8- × 8-inch pan sprayed with non-stick spray. Bake for 30–35 minutes, until golden and the top springs back when lightly touched. Cool in the pan on a wire rack. Once completely cool, frost with Maple or Brown Sugar Frosting.

Makes 12 bars.

Apple, Cranberry & Walnut Bars with Lemon Cream Cheese Frosting

Add ½ cup dried cranberries and ⅓ cup chopped walnuts to the batter along with the apples. Spread with Lemon Cream Cheese Frosting (page 198). Adds 2 g fat per bar.

Chunky Lemon Pear Bars

Replace the applesauce with drained, mashed canned pears, and use chopped, peeled pears in place of the apples. Add the grated zest of a lemon to the egg-sugar-butter mixture too. Fat content remains the same.

Spiced Zucchini Bars with Cranberries & Pecans

These are very similar to carrot cake. If you want to boost vitamins, add a big spoonful of tomato paste, which after all is a fruit, to the butter-sugar-egg mixture. Don't peel your zucchini before eating or baking with them: most of the nutritional benefits come from the skin, which is rich in beta carotene.

Preheat the oven to 350°F.

In a large bowl, beat the butter, brown sugar, egg and vanilla with an electric mixer or by hand until smooth.

In a medium bowl, combine the flour, baking soda, cinnamon, allspice and salt. Add the flour mixture and zucchini to the egg mixture, stirring by hand until almost combined. Add the cranberries and pecans and stir just until blended.

Spread the batter into an 8- × 8-inch pan sprayed with non-stick spray. Bake for 25–30 minutes, until the top is springy to the touch. Cool in the pan on a wire rack.

Makes 12 bars.

Ingredients

3 Tbsp butter or non-hydrogenated margarine, softened
¾ cup packed brown sugar
1 large egg
1 tsp vanilla
1 cup all-purpose or whole wheat flour
1 tsp baking soda
½ tsp cinnamon
¼ tsp allspice
¼ tsp salt
1 cup packed grated raw, unpeeled zucchini (about 1)
½ cup dried cranberries or raisins
¼ cup chopped pecans
Lemon Cream Cheese Frosting (optional, see page 198)

Nutrition Facts
Per bar

Calories	145
Fat	4.9 g
Saturated	2 g
Monounsaturated	1.3 g
Polyunsaturated	1.2 g
Carbohydrates	23.3 g
Cholesterol	25.7 mg
Protein	2.4 g
Fiber	1.1 g
Calories from fat	30%

Easy Cocoa Brownies

Peanut Butter Swirl Brownies

The Ultimate Fudge Brownies

Rocky Road Brownies

Marshmallow Macaroon Brownies

Turtle Brownies

Chocolate Chip Zucchini Brownies

Cheesecake Brownies

Coffee White Chocolate Chunk Blondies

Peanut Butter Blondies

Turtle Blondies

Blondies Five Ways

Brownies

Easy Cocoa Brownies

These are the easiest brownies you'll ever make from scratch. The addition of coffee doesn't give them a mocha flavor, but rather enhances the chocolate without adding any fat. Remember not to overbake them. The edges should start pulling away from the sides of the pan, but the middle should still be soft; it will firm up as it cools.

Preheat the oven to 350°F.

In a large bowl, stir together the butter and sugar. Add the eggs, vanilla and coffee and stir until well blended and smooth.

In a small bowl, combine the flour, cocoa, baking powder and salt. Add to the egg mixture and stir by hand just until blended.

Spread the batter into an 8- × 8-inch pan sprayed with non-stick spray. Bake for 25–30 minutes, until the edges just begin to pull away from the sides of the pan, but the middle is still slightly soft. Don't overbake! Cool in the pan on a wire rack.

Makes 16 brownies.

Chocolate Nut Brownies
Stir ⅓ cup chopped toasted walnuts, pecans or other nuts into the brownie batter just before spreading in the pan. Adds 1.3 g fat per brownie.

Chocolate Chip Brownies
Stir ½ cup chocolate chips or chunks into the batter before spreading in the pan. Adds 2 g fat per brownie.

Inside-Out Brownies
Stir ½ cup chopped white chocolate into the batter before spreading in the pan. Adds 2 g fat per brownie.

Ingredients

¼ cup butter or non-hydrogenated margarine, melted
1¼ cups sugar
2 large eggs
1 tsp vanilla
1 tsp instant coffee granules,
  dissolved in 1 tsp water
1 cup all-purpose flour
½ cup cocoa
¼ tsp baking powder
¼ tsp salt

Nutrition Facts
Per brownie

Calories	115
Fat	3.4 g
Saturated	1.9 g
Monounsaturated	1 g
Polyunsaturated	0.2 g
Carbohydrates	20.7 g
Cholesterol	30.8 mg
Protein	2 g
Fiber	1.3 g
Calories from fat	25%

Peanut Butter Swirl Brownies

If there was ever a brownie that begged for a glass of milk, this is it.

Preheat the oven to 350°F.

In a large bowl, mix together the butter and sugar by hand until well combined. Add the egg, vanilla and coffee. Stir until thoroughly blended and smooth.

In a medium bowl, combine the flour, cocoa, baking powder and salt. Add to the egg mixture and stir by hand just until combined. Spread the batter into an 8- × 8-inch pan sprayed with non-stick spray.

In a medium bowl, combine the peanut butter, brown sugar, egg white, milk, vanilla and flour and stir until smooth. Drop in large spoonfuls over the top of the brownie batter, and draw the tip of a knife through both batters to create a marbled effect.

Bake for 35–40 minutes, until the edges begin to pull away from the sides of the pan but the middle is still slightly soft. Don't overbake. Cool in the pan on a wire rack.

Makes 16 brownies.

Ingredients

¼ cup butter or non-hydrogenated margarine, melted
1¼ cups sugar
2 large eggs
1 tsp vanilla
1 tsp instant coffee granules, dissolved in 1 tsp water
1 cup all-purpose flour
½ cup cocoa
¼ tsp baking powder
¼ tsp salt

Topping
½ cup light or all-natural peanut butter
⅓ cup packed brown sugar
1 large egg white
2 Tbsp milk
¼ tsp vanilla
1 Tbsp all-purpose flour

Nutrition Facts
Per brownie

Calories	188
Fat	6.6 g
Saturated	2.6 g
Monounsaturated	2.4 g
Polyunsaturated	1.2 g
Carbohydrates	30.8 g
Cholesterol	34.8 mg
Protein	4 g
Fiber	1.5 g
Calories from fat	30%

Ingredients

¼ cup butter or non-hydrogenated margarine
1 oz unsweetened chocolate
   (1 square)
⅔ cup cocoa
1½ cups sugar
1 large egg
2 large egg whites
1 tsp instant coffee granules,
   dissolved in 1 tsp water
1 tsp vanilla
1 cup all-purpose flour
½ tsp baking powder
¼ tsp salt

Nutrition Facts

Per brownie

Calories	150
Fat	4.5 g
Saturated	2.6 g
Monounsaturated	1.4 g
Polyunsaturated	0.2 g
Carbohydrates	27.4 g
Cholesterol	21.2 mg
Protein	2.6 g
Fiber	2.2 g
Calories from fat	25%

The Ultimate Fudge Brownies

My grandma used to make brownies that were fudgy on the inside, with an intensely chocolate flavor and crackling top. This is the closest I've come without using a cup of butter. The large quantity of cocoa gives them a deep chocolate flavor without adding fat.

Preheat the oven to 350°F.

In a medium saucepan, melt the butter and chocolate over medium-low heat, stirring often. Remove from the heat and stir in the cocoa and sugar. Mix until well blended. It will have the consistency of very wet sand.

In a large bowl, whisk together the egg, egg whites, coffee and vanilla. Add the chocolate mixture and mix until well blended and smooth.

In a small bowl, stir together the flour, baking powder and salt; add to the chocolate mixture and stir just until combined.

Pour into an 8- × 8-inch pan sprayed with non-stick spray. Bake for 25–30 minutes, until set around the edges but still slightly soft in the middle. They'll seem to be not quite cooked, but will set a little more as they cool. Don't overbake! Cool in the pan on a wire rack.

Makes 16 brownies.

Oreo Brownies

Chop 6 Oreo cookies into quarters and gently press into the top of the batter before baking. Adds less than 1 g fat per brownie.

Mint Brownies

Coarsely chop 2 small boxes of Junior Mints or 2 Peppermint Patties. This is easier if they're frozen first. Stir into the batter before spreading in the pan and bake as directed. Adds half a gram of fat per brownie.

Caramel Pecan Brownies

Coarsely chop 1 pkg Rolo chocolate-covered caramels or 1 Caramilk bar and sprinkle it over the brownie batter along with ¼ cup chopped pecans. Drizzle with 2 Tbsp caramel or butterscotch topping before you bake them. Adds 2 g fat per brownie.

Ingredients

1½ cups all-purpose flour
1½ cups packed brown sugar
½ cup cocoa
1 tsp baking powder
½ tsp baking soda
¼ tsp salt
¼ cup canola oil
¼ cup chocolate syrup (such as Hershey's or Nesquik)
1 cup milk
1 tsp instant coffee granules
2 large eggs
1 tsp vanilla
½ cup chocolate chips
⅓ cup chopped pecans or walnuts
1–2 cups mini marshmallows

Nutrition Facts

Per brownie

Calories	204
Fat	7 g
Saturated	1.9 g
Monounsaturated	3.2 g
Polyunsaturated	1.6 g
Carbohydrates	34 g
Cholesterol	23 mg
Protein	3.2 g
Fiber	1.8 g
Calories from fat	30%

Rocky Road Brownies

Halfway between chocolate cake and cake-like brownies, these are loaded with chocolate chips and nuts and topped with a gooey jumble of marshmallows and chocolate crumble. Toast the nuts in a dry frying pan first if you want to maximize their flavor.

Preheat the oven to 350°F.

In a large bowl, stir together the flour, brown sugar, cocoa, baking powder, baking soda and salt. Add the canola oil and chocolate syrup and stir with a fork until the mixture is crumbly. Blend with your fingers until the ingredients are evenly combined and have the consistency of damp soil. Remove about a cup of the mixture and set it aside.

In a medium bowl, stir together the milk, coffee, eggs and vanilla. Add to the crumb mixture and stir just until blended. The mixture will be wet with some small lumps; don't worry about getting all the lumps out. Stir in the chocolate chips, walnuts and marshmallows.

Pour the batter into a 9- × 13-inch pan sprayed with non-stick spray and sprinkle with the reserved crumb mixture.

Bake for 30 minutes, until the edges are set but the middle is still soft, and a toothpick inserted comes out with some crumbs stuck to it. If the marshmallows, which will rise to the top, are darkening too quickly, cover loosely with a piece of aluminum foil. Cool in the pan on a wire rack.

Makes 20 brownies.

Marshmallow Macaroon Brownies

This is a three-tiered brownie with a chewy coconut base, fudgy middle and toasted marshmallows on top. No one will believe they contain only a tablespoon of butter.

Preheat the oven to 350°F.

In a large bowl, combine the egg, brown sugar and vanilla and mix until well blended and smooth.

In a small bowl, combine the flour, baking powder, and salt. Add the dry ingredients to the egg mixture and stir just until combined.

Transfer half the batter into a medium bowl and set it aside. Stir the coconut into the remaining batter and spread evenly in an 8- × 8-inch pan sprayed with non-stick spray. Add the cocoa, butter and nuts to the batter you set aside and stir just until blended. With a spatula, gently spread the chocolate batter over the coconut batter.

Bake for 25–30 minutes, until just set. Remove from the oven and sprinkle the marshmallows over top of the brownies. Return to the oven for 2–5 minutes, until they are pale golden and puffed. Cool completely in the pan on a wire rack.

Makes 16 brownies.

Ingredients

2 large eggs
¾ cup packed brown sugar
1 tsp vanilla
¾ cup all-purpose flour
½ tsp baking powder
¼ tsp salt
½ cup shredded coconut (sweetened or unsweetened)
¼ cup cocoa
1 Tbsp butter or non-hydrogenated margarine, melted
¼ cup chopped walnuts or pecans
1½ cups mini marshmallows

Nutrition Facts
Per brownie

Calories	116
Fat	3.4 g
Saturated	1.5 g
Monounsaturated	0.8 g
Polyunsaturated	0.9 g
Carbohydrates	20.3 g
Cholesterol	29 mg
Protein	2.3 g
Fiber	1.3 g
Calories from fat	25%

Ingredients

¼ cup butter or non-hydrogenated margarine, melted
1¼ cups sugar
1 large egg
2 large egg whites
1 tsp vanilla
1 tsp instant coffee powder,
   dissolved in 1 tsp water
1 cup all-purpose flour
½ cup cocoa
¼ tsp baking powder
¼ tsp salt
Filling
15 caramels, unwrapped
1 Tbsp milk
¼ cup chopped pecans

Nutrition Facts
Per brownie

Calories	167
Fat	5.2 g
Saturated	2.6 g
Monounsaturated	1.8 g
Polyunsaturated	0.5 g
Carbohydrates	29.4 g
Cholesterol	21.8 mg
Protein	2.7 g
Fiber	1.7 g
Calories from fat	27%

Turtle Brownies

Everything you could ever want in a brownie is right here in this recipe. The middle oozes with a layer of rich caramel and crunchy pecans.

Preheat the oven to 350°F.

In a large bowl, mix the butter and sugar until well combined. Add the egg, egg whites, vanilla and coffee and stir until thoroughly blended and smooth.

In a medium bowl, combine the flour, cocoa, baking powder and salt. Add to the egg mixture and stir by hand just until combined.

Spread half of the batter into an 8- × 8-inch pan sprayed with non-stick spray, and bake for 10 minutes. Meanwhile, melt the caramels with the milk in a small bowl in the microwave for 1–2 minutes, stirring once or twice.

Drizzle the melted caramel over the partially baked brownies, and sprinkle with pecans. Drop the remaining batter in spoonfuls evenly over the top. Spread gently over the caramel, but don't worry about covering it evenly or completely.

Bake for 30–35 minutes, until the edges just begin to pull away from the sides of the pan, but the middle is still slightly soft. Don't overbake! Cool in the pan on a wire rack.

Makes 16 brownies.

Chocolate Chip Zucchini Brownies

If I have to eat zucchini, I want it to be wrapped up in a brownie. Because it has some texture to it, this is a perfect recipe to add a sprinkle of ground flaxseed to.

Preheat the oven to 350°F.

In a large bowl, combine the flours, cocoa, baking powder and salt; set aside.

In a medium bowl, stir together the melted butter, sugar, brown sugar, eggs and vanilla until smooth. Add the egg mixture and the zucchini to the flour mixture and stir by hand until almost combined; add the chocolate chips and flaxseed and stir just until blended.

Pour into an 8- × 8-inch pan sprayed with non-stick spray. Bake for 30–35 minutes, until the edges are springy to the touch but the middle is still slightly soft. A slight indentation should be left when touched. Don't overbake! Cool in the pan on a wire rack or eat them warm from the pan.

Makes 12 brownies.

Ingredients

½ cup all-purpose flour
½ cup whole wheat flour
½ cup cocoa
½ tsp baking powder
¼ tsp salt
¼ cup butter or non-hydroge-nated margarine, melted, or canola oil
½ cup sugar
½ cup packed brown sugar
2 large eggs
1 tsp vanilla
1 packed cup grated raw, un-peeled zucchini (1 medium)
⅓ cup chocolate chips
2 Tbsp ground flaxseed (optional)

Nutrition Facts
Per brownie

Calories	147
Fat	5.1 g
Saturated	2.9 g
Monounsaturated	1.5 g
Polyunsaturated	0.4 g
Carbohydrates	24.4 g
Cholesterol	35 mg
Protein	2.8 g
Fiber	2.5 g
Calories from fat	30%

Ingredients

1 cup all-purpose flour
½ cup cocoa
¼ tsp baking powder
¼ tsp salt
¼ cup butter or non-hydroge-
    nated margarine, melted
1¼ cups sugar
1 large egg
2 large egg whites
1 tsp instant coffee powder,
    dissolved in 1 tsp water
1 tsp vanilla
Cheesecake Topping
one 8-oz pkg light cream
    cheese
⅓ cup sugar
1 tsp vanilla
1 large egg white
1 Tbsp all-purpose flour

Nutrition Facts

Per brownie

Calories	178
Fat	6.2 g
Saturated	3.6 g
Monounsaturated	1.9 g
Polyunsaturated	0.3 g
Carbohydrates	28.4 g
Cholesterol	30.2 mg
Protein	3.8 g
Fiber	1.5 g
Calories from fat	30%

Cheesecake Brownies

Try baking these in an 8-inch or 9-inch round cake pan and then serving them in wedges topped with fresh berries or thawed frozen berries in syrup.

Preheat the oven to 350°F.

In a small bowl, stir together the flour, cocoa, baking powder and salt; set aside.

In a large bowl, stir together the butter and sugar. Add the egg, egg whites, coffee and vanilla and stir until well blended and smooth. Add the flour mixture and stir by hand just until blended. Spread about two thirds of the batter into an 8- × 8-inch pan sprayed with non-stick spray.

To make the topping, beat the cream cheese with an electric mixer in a small bowl until smooth and creamy. Add the sugar and vanilla and beat for a minute or two, until very smooth. Add the egg white and flour and beat again just until combined.

Pour the cheesecake topping over the batter and spread it evenly to the edges. Drop spoonfuls of the remaining brownie batter over the cheesecake layer, and use the tip of a knife to gently swirl the surface and create a marbled effect.

Bake for 30–35 minutes, until golden and the top springs back when lightly touched. Don't overbake. Cool in the pan on a wire rack.

Makes 16 brownies.

Raspberry Cheesecake Brownies

Drop ¼ cup raspberry or cherry jam in spoonfuls evenly over the top of the cheesecake batter along with the brownie batter. Draw the tip of a knife through the jam and both batters to create a marbled effect. Fat content remains the same.

Coffee White Chocolate Chunk Blondies

Creamy white chocolate goes so well with coffee-flavored brownies, but semi-sweet or dark chocolate is just as delicious.

When in doubt, underbake your brownies rather than overbake them—brownies of all varieties have the best texture when they are dense, moist and chewy, which is often ruined by overbaking. You can tell they are done when the edges just begin to pull away from the sides of the pan. The top should not be springy to the touch (as a cake would be), and if you stick a toothpick in, it should come out not completely gooey and covered with batter, but with plenty of moist crumbs sticking to it.

Preheat oven to 350°F.

In a small saucepan, combine the butter, brown sugar and instant coffee. Cook over medium heat, stirring often, until the butter melts and the mixture is smooth. Transfer to a medium bowl and let it cool down a bit.

Add the egg, egg white and vanilla to the brown sugar mixture and stir until well blended and smooth. Sprinkle the flour, baking powder and salt overtop and stir by hand until almost combined; add the white chocolate and stir just until blended.

Spread the batter into an 8- × 8-inch pan that has been sprayed with nonstick spray. Bake for 25–30 minutes, until the edges are pale golden and just starting to pull away from the sides of the pan. Cool in the pan on a wire rack.

Makes 16 blondies.

Chocolate Mocha Brownies
Stir ¼ cup cocoa into the flour before adding it. Fat content remains the same.

Ingredients

¼ cup butter or non-hydrogenated margarine
1 cup packed brown sugar
1 Tbsp instant coffee or espresso
1 large egg
1 large egg white
1 tsp vanilla
1 cup all-purpose flour
1 tsp baking powder
¼ tsp salt
½ cup white chocolate chips or chunks

Nutrition Facts
Per blondie

Calories	141
Fat	4.9 g
Saturated	2.8 g
Monounsaturated	1.5 g
Polyunsaturated	0.2 g
Carbohydrates	22.8 g
Cholesterol	22.4 mg
Fiber	0.2 g
Calories from fat	31%

Peanut Butter Blondies

You can pretend you're making these for the kids, but really they're for grown-ups, who love them just as much eaten warm, straight from the pan.

Preheat the oven to 350°F.

In a large bowl, combine the peanut butter, sugar, brown sugar, egg, egg white, oil and vanilla. Stir until well blended and smooth.

In a small bowl, combine the flour, baking soda and salt. Add to the peanut butter mixture and stir by hand until almost combined. Add the peanut butter chips and stir just until blended.

Spread batter into an 8- × 8-inch pan that has been sprayed with non-stick spray. Bake for 25–28 minutes, until golden and set around the edges but still soft in the middle. Cool in the pan on a wire rack.

Makes 16 brownies.

Ingredients

½ cup light or all-natural
   peanut butter
½ cup sugar
½ cup packed brown sugar
1 large egg
1 large egg white
1 Tbsp canola oil
1 tsp vanilla
½ cup all-purpose flour
½ cup whole wheat flour
¼ tsp baking soda
¼ tsp salt
⅓ cup butterscotch or chocolate chips

Nutrition Facts
Per blondie

Calories	135
Fat	4.2 g
Saturated	1.4 g
Monounsaturated	1.6 g
Polyunsaturated	1 g
Carbohydrates	22.8 g
Cholesterol	13.5 mg
Protein	2.6 g
Fiber	0.6 g
Calories from fat	27%

Turtle Blondies

If you love blondies but miss the chocolate, sneak some back into its midsection, with a jumble of caramel and nuts, just to be on the safe side.

Preheat the oven to 350°F.

In a large bowl, combine the melted butter and brown sugar; mix well. Add the egg whites and vanilla and stir until well blended and smooth.

In a small bowl, combine the flour, baking powder and salt. Add to the sugar mixture and stir by hand just until combined.

Spread half the batter into an 8- × 8-inch pan sprayed with non-stick spray. Bake for 10 minutes. Meanwhile, combine the caramels and milk in a small microwave-safe bowl. Heat on medium power in the microwave for 1–2 minutes, until melted and smooth, stirring once or twice.

Drizzle the caramel over the partially baked blondies, sprinkle with chocolate chips and nuts, and drop the remaining batter in spoonfuls over top. Spread gently over the caramel, but don't worry about covering it evenly or completely.

Return to the oven for 25–30 minutes, until the edges are barely golden and start to pull away from the sides of the pan. Cool in the pan on a wire rack.

Makes 16 blondies.

Ingredients

¼ cup butter or non-hydrogenated margarine, melted
1⅓ cups packed brown sugar
2 large egg whites or 1 large egg
1 tsp vanilla
1 cup all-purpose flour
1 tsp baking powder
¼ tsp salt

Filling

15 regular or chocolate caramels, unwrapped
1 Tbsp milk
¼ cup chocolate chips
¼ cup chopped walnuts or pecans

Nutrition Facts

Per blondie

Calories	187
Fat	5.7 g
Saturated	3 g
Monounsaturated	1.4 g
Polyunsaturated	1 g
Carbohydrates	32.5 g
Cholesterol	8.6 mg
Protein	2.4 g
Fiber	0.7 g
Calories from fat	27%

Ingredients

¼ cup butter or non-hydroge-
    nated margarine, melted
1⅓ cups packed brown sugar
1 large egg or 2 large egg
    whites
2 tsp vanilla
1 cup all-purpose flour
1 tsp baking powder
¼ tsp salt
¼ cup chopped walnuts or
    pecans

Nutrition Facts

Per blondie

Calories	141
Fat	4.4 g
Saturated	1 g
Monounsaturated	1.2 g
Polyunsaturated	0.9 g
Carbohydrates	24.2 g
Cholesterol	21.2 mg
Protein	1.7 g
Fiber	0.3 g
Calories from fat	28%

Blondies Five Ways

A blondie is first cousin to the brownie, but no less delicious if not as famous. A blondie contains no chocolate, but has the same dense richness and texture as a brownie, typically made possible by chewy, caramelly brown sugar. Here are five ways to dress them up: with nuts, with lime and white chocolate, with dried cranberries and white chocolate, with pecan halves or with a gooey rocky road topping.

Preheat the oven to 350°F.

In a large bowl, stir together the melted butter and brown sugar. Add egg whites and vanilla and stir until well blended and smooth.

In a small bowl, combine the flour, baking powder, salt and nuts. Add to the sugar mixture and stir by hand just until combined.

Spread the batter into an 8- × 8-inch pan sprayed with non-stick spray. Bake for 25–30 minutes, until the edges are barely golden and start to pull away from the sides of the pan. Cool in the pan on a wire rack.

Makes 16 blondies.

Lime & White Chocolate Chunk Blondies

Add the grated zest and juice of a lime or two to the butter-brown sugar mixture, and ½ cup chopped white chocolate instead of the nuts. Adds half a gram of fat per blondie.

Cranberry White Chocolate Chunk Blondies

Add ½ cup chopped white chocolate and ¼ cup dried cranberries instead of the nuts. Adds half a gram of fat per blondie.

Rocky Road Blondies

Mix and bake the blondies as directed, reserving the nuts to sprinkle on top instead. When the pan comes out of the oven, sprinkle with 2 cups mini marshmallows, ⅓ cup chocolate chips and the nuts. Return to the oven for 5–7 minutes, or until the marshmallows are slightly puffed. Let cool in the pan on a wire rack. Adds 1 g fat per blondie.

Two-Bite Pecan Blondies

Omit the walnuts and divide the batter among 16 mini muffin tins that have been sprayed with non-stick spray. Press a pecan half into the top of each and bake for 20–25 minutes. Adds 1 g fat per blondie, but only the good kind.

Rice Krispies Squares

Peanut Butter & Honey Crunch Seed Bars

Puffed Wheat Squares

Power Balls (a.k.a. Chocolate Satellites)

Crispy Chocolate Peanut Butter Bars

Those No-Bake Chocolate Oatmeal Cookies

Crispy Chewy Fruit & Honey Granola Bars

Nanaimo Bars

White Chocolate Truffles

No-Bake

Ingredients

3 Tbsp butter or non-hydroge-
    nated margarine
one 250-g pkg (about 40)
    regular marshmallows (or 4
    cups mini marshmallows)
6 cups Rice Krispies cereal

Nutrition Facts

Per square

Calories	86
Fat	1.8 g
Saturated	1.1 g
Monounsaturated	0.5 g
Polyunsaturated	0.1 g
Carbohydrates	17 g
Cholesterol	4.7 mg
Protein	0.8 g
Fiber	0.1 g
Calories from fat	19%

Rice Krispies Squares

Did you know that the most popular No-Bake cookie of all time is also low in fat? The wonderful thing about these crispy-chewy treats is that they're so versatile—try using other cereals instead of or as well as Rice Krispies: puffed wheat, Cheerios, Special K, bran flakes and even popcorn all work well. Stir in chopped dried fruit, nuts, seeds, oats, chocolate or peanut butter chips, candies, mini marshmallows, chopped caramels or Tootsie Rolls, low-fat granola, crumbled cookies or graham crackers—anything you can think of! They're even better for you made with non-hydrogenated margarine.

In a large saucepan, melt the butter over medium-low heat. Add the marshmallows and stir until melted and smooth.

Remove from the heat and stir in the cereal. Mix until well coated. Press into a 9- × 13-inch pan sprayed with non-stick spray. Cool in the fridge or at room temperature.

Cut into 20 squares.

Peanut Butter Rice Krispies Squares

Stir ½ cup light peanut butter into the marshmallow mixture as soon as you take it off the heat. Adds 1.5 g fat per square.

Caramel Rice Krispies Squares

Melt ½ cup caramel or butterscotch topping along with the butter and marshmallows. Fat content remains the same.

Chocolate or Butterscotch Rice Krispies Squares

Add ¼ cup dry chocolate or butterscotch pudding mix and 1 tsp vanilla to the butter-marshmallow mixture as soon as you take it off the heat. Fat content remains the same.

Peanut Butter & Honey Crunch Seed Bars

There are a lot of packaged bars on the market like these; often they have various kinds of seeds added, and you can add a combination of any you like. Pumpkin seeds are very high in protein and are lower in fat; sunflower and sesame seeds are high in fiber and all are great sources of healthy mono- and polyunsaturated fats.

Spray the inside of a large bowl with non-stick spray. Combine the corn flakes, bran flakes and seeds in the bowl and set aside.

In a small saucepan, combine the peanut butter, brown sugar and honey. Cook over medium heat, stirring frequently, until completely melted and smooth. Remove from the heat and stir in the vanilla.

Pour over the cereal and gently stir to coat well. Press the mixture into an ungreased 8- × 8-inch pan and chill until firm before cutting into bars.

Makes 12 bars.

Ingredients

2½ cups corn flakes
2½ cups bran flakes
¼ cup sunflower seeds
¼ cup sesame seeds
   (optional)
½ cup light or all-natural
   peanut butter
½ cup packed brown sugar
¼ cup honey or maple syrup
½ tsp vanilla

Nutrition Facts
Per bar

Calories	229
Fat	5.2 g
Saturated	0.8 g
Monounsaturated	1.9 g
Polyunsaturated	2.1 g
Carbohydrates	43.7 g
Cholesterol	0 mg
Protein	4.7 g
Fiber	2.1 g
Calories from fat	19%

Ingredients

¼ cup butter or non-hydroge-
    nated margarine
½ cup corn syrup
1 cup packed brown sugar
3 Tbsp cocoa
1 tsp vanilla
8 cups puffed wheat

Nutrition Facts

Per square

Calories	106
Fat	2.4 g
Saturated	1.5 g
Monounsaturated	0.7 g
Polyunsaturated	0.1 g
Carbohydrates	21.2 g
Cholesterol	6.2 mg
Protein	0.9 g
Fiber	0.6 g
Calories from fat	20%

Puffed Wheat Squares

These satisfy my cravings for something crunchy, chewy and chocolatey all at once—the quintessential snack, in my mind. They aren't as high in fiber as you'd think, considering they're made with puffed wheat, but they're easy to sneak some ground flaxseed into.

Lightly spray the inside of a large bowl with non-stick spray. Put the puffed wheat into the bowl and set it aside.

In a small saucepan, combine the butter, corn syrup, brown sugar and cocoa over medium heat. Bring to a boil, stirring frequently.

Remove from the heat and stir in the vanilla. Pour over the puffed wheat and stir to coat evenly. Press into an ungreased 9- × 13-inch pan and refrigerate or leave at room temperature until set. These are easiest to cut at room temperature.

Makes 20 squares.

Buttery Chocolate "Popcorn" Squares
Replace the puffed wheat with an equal amount of Corn Pops cereal. Fat content remains the same.

Power Balls (a.k.a. Chocolate Satellites)

During the 2 years I lived in Vancouver, I was hooked on those Coco Orbs at Capers markets. When I arrived back in Calgary, I was determined to recreate them on my own. These are similar but contain pumpkin seeds and soy milk for added protein and flaxseed because I love to add flax to anything I can.

If you're using old-fashioned (large flake) oats, pulse them a few times in the food processor to grind them up a bit. If you're using quick oats, don't worry about it.

In a large bowl, toss together the oats, rice cakes, dried fruit, coconut, pumpkin seeds, flaxseed and salt. In a small saucepan, combine the cocoa, peanut butter and maple syrup and set over medium heat. Cook until melted and smooth, stirring often. Remove from the heat and stir in the soy milk until well blended and smooth.

Pour the chocolate mixture over the dry ingredients and stir until well combined. Put the bowl in the fridge until the mixture is cool. Shape into balls the size of those large bouncy balls — bigger than a golf ball, smaller than a baseball. Store them covered, in the fridge.

Makes 1 dozen balls.

Ingredients

1 cup oats
5 brown rice cakes, crumbled
1 cup chopped dried fruit (such as apricots, cranberries, raisins, figs, blueberries)
½ cup shredded coconut
½ cup pumpkin seeds, chopped or pulsed in the food processor
¼ cup ground flaxseed and/or sunflower seeds
pinch salt
½ cup cocoa
½ cup light or all-natural peanut butter
½ cup maple syrup
½ cup soy milk or regular milk

Nutrition Facts
Per ball

Calories	225
Fat	7.6 g
Saturated	2.1 g
Monounsaturated	2.4 g
Polyunsaturated	2.6 g
Carbohydrates	37.6 g
Cholesterol	0 mg
Protein	6 g
Fiber	4.3 g
Calories from fat	28%

Crispy Chocolate Peanut Butter Bars

Everyone says these chewy, chocolatey treats taste like Eat-More bars. But these have the added benefit of vitamins, minerals and fiber, and most of the fat is unsaturated, so you can eat more of them. They keep and travel well—ideal for wrapping individually to take with you.

In a large bowl, toss together the cereal, oats, dried fruit, peanuts and flaxseed.

In a small saucepan, combine the brown sugar, cocoa, peanut butter and honey over medium heat and stir until completely melted and smooth. (Alternatively, you could do this in the microwave.) Pour over the fruit and cereal mixture and stir until evenly coated.

Press into a 9- × 13-inch pan and chill until firm, before cutting into bars.

Makes 18 bars.

Ingredients

3 cups Rice Krispies or Special K cereal
1 cup oats
1 cup chopped dried fruit (such as raisins, cranberries & apricots)
½ cup chopped peanuts
¼ cup ground flaxseed (optional)
½ cup packed brown sugar
½ cup cocoa
½ cup light or all-natural peanut butter
½ cup honey

Nutrition Facts

Per bar

Calories	173
Fat	5.1 g
Saturated	0.9 g
Monounsaturated	2.3 g
Polyunsaturated	1.6 g
Carbohydrates	31.3 g
Cholesterol	0 mg
Protein	4.1 g
Fiber	2.6 g
Calories from fat	25%

Those No-Bake Chocolate Oatmeal Cookies

This is a lightened version of those old-fashioned no-bake cookie balls your elderly relatives probably used to make. If you like, the mixture can be simply dropped by the spoonful onto waxed paper while still soft instead of rolled into balls. For something a little more indulgent, increase the amount of nuts and replace the chopped fruit with chopped white or dark chocolate.

In a medium-large saucepan, combine the sugar, milk and butter in a medium-large saucepan and bring to a full boil over medium heat. Reduce the heat and simmer for 3 minutes, stirring frequently.

Remove from the heat and stir in the vanilla, cocoa, oats, fruit and nuts. Chill the mixture for about an hour, or until firm.

Shape the mixture into 1-inch balls and roll in icing sugar to coat. Chill until firm. Store in a covered container in the refrigerator or at room temperature. If the cookies start to absorb some of the icing sugar, simply re-roll them.

Makes 20 cookies.

Ingredients

1 cup sugar
⅓ cup milk
2 Tbsp butter or non-hydrogenated margarine
½ tsp vanilla
⅓ cup cocoa
1 cup quick oats
¼ cup packed finely chopped dried fruit (such as cranberries, apricots and/or cherries)
¼ cup finely chopped walnuts, pecans or almonds, toasted if you like
¼ cup shredded coconut
icing sugar, for rolling (optional)

Nutrition Facts

Per cookie

Calories	93
Fat	2.8 g
Saturated	1.2 g
Monounsaturated	0.7 g
Polyunsaturated	0.8 g
Carbohydrates	16.6 g
Cholesterol	3.3 mg
Protein	1.6 g
Fiber	1.4 g
Calories from fat	26%

Ingredients

1 Tbsp butter or non-hydrogenated margarine
¼ cup packed brown sugar
¼ cup honey
¼ tsp cinnamon
pinch salt
1 cup chopped dried fruit
(such as raisins, apricots,
cranberries, cherries and/or
dates)
1½ cups Rice Krispies cereal
1 cup quick oats
1 Tbsp ground flaxseed
(optional)

Nutrition Facts

Per bar

Calories	120
Fat	1.6 g
Saturated	0.7 g
Monounsaturated	0.5 g
Polyunsaturated	0.2 g
Carbohydrates	26 g
Cholesterol	2.6 mg
Protein	1.8 g
Fiber	1.6 g
Calories from fat	11%

Crispy Chewy Fruit & Honey Granola Bars

These are like those individually packaged chewy granola bars you can buy at the grocery store. Not only do these taste better and cost less, they contain less sugar, no preservatives, and more fiber and other good stuff from the dried fruit and oats.

In a medium-large saucepan, combine the butter, brown sugar, honey, cinnamon and salt. Bring to a boil over medium heat and cook, stirring frequently, for 1 minute.

Remove from heat and stir in the fruit, cereal and oats. Press the mixture into an ungreased 8- × 8-inch pan and refrigerate or leave at room temperature until firm.

Makes 12 bars.

Chewy Marshmallow Chocolate Chip Granola Bars

Omit the cinnamon and dried fruit. Stir the cereal and oats into the honey mixture as directed, transfer to a bowl and set aside to cool slightly. When the mixture is almost at room temperature, stir in ⅓ cup coarsely chopped chocolate chips and 1 generous cup mini marshmallows. Press into the pan and chill until set. Adds 1.4 g fat per bar.

Toasted Nut & Seed Granola Bars

Omit the cinnamon and dried fruit. Toast the oatmeal in a dry pan until pale golden and fragrant. Toast ½ cup chopped walnuts, pecans, hazelnuts or almonds with ¼ cup sunflower seeds the same way, and add the toasted oatmeal, nuts and seeds and 2 Tbsp ground flaxseed to the syrup mixture along with the cereal and proceed as directed. Adds 4.3 g fat per bar.

Caramel Apple Granola Bars

Replace the dried fruit with finely chopped dried apples. Stir the cereal and oats into the honey mixture as directed, transfer to a bowl and set aside to cool for about 15 minutes. When the mixture is almost at room temperature, stir in ½ cup butterscotch chips. Adds 1.5 g fat per bar.

Nanaimo Bars

When I was a kid, I obsessed about Nanaimo bars and butter tarts, and to this day I get giddy if I see some on a plate of dainties. This was also the toughest recipe in this book to reduce the fat in; in fact I gave up twice, but I'm glad I persisted.

For the record, these originated in Nanaimo, BC, although you'll see versions in US cookbooks labeled "New York Slice." Custard powder can be found in tins alongside the pudding at the grocery store.

In the bowl of a double boiler or a medium stainless steel bowl, combine the brown sugar, cocoa, butter and corn syrup. Stir in the egg and set over a pot of simmering water; whisk until the mixture melts and thickens slightly. Remove from the heat and stir in the vanilla, graham crumbs, coconut and salt.

Press the mixture firmly into the bottom of an ungreased 8- × 8-inch pan and pop it in the freezer while making the filling.

In a medium bowl, beat the butter, custard powder, icing sugar, milk and vanilla until creamy and smooth, adding a few extra drops of milk if necessary until you have a spreadable frosting. Spread over the base. Return to the freezer or fridge to chill until firm, before covering with chocolate.

Melt the chocolate in a medium bowl set over hot water, or on medium power in the microwave. Stir until smooth and spread over the filling. Refrigerate until well chilled and firm. These are easiest to cut at room temperature, using a small, sharp, serrated knife, so pull them out of the fridge and set them on the countertop for about ½ hour before you plan to eat them.

Makes 20 bars.

Ingredients

Base

¼ cup packed brown sugar
¼ cup cocoa
3 Tbsp butter
3 Tbsp corn syrup
1 large egg or egg white
½ tsp vanilla
2 cups graham wafer crumbs
⅓ cup shredded coconut
pinch salt

Filling

3 Tbsp butter, softened
3 Tbsp custard powder
2 cups icing sugar
2 Tbsp milk
1 tsp vanilla

Topping

1 cup chocolate chips

Nutrition Facts

Per bar

Calories	213
Fat	8.3 g
Saturated	4.8 g
Monounsaturated	2.3 g
Polyunsaturated	0.9 g
Carbohydrates	33.8 g
Cholesterol	21 mg
Protein	2 g
Fiber	1.6 g
Calories from fat	34%

White Chocolate Truffles

Most chocolate truffles are delicious combinations of chocolate, cream and often butter, making them very high in fat and calories. The light cream cheese makes these much lower in fat with a smooth and creamy mouthfeel, and because the mixture isn't hot or temperamental to work with, it's a great recipe for kids to make.

Place the chocolate in a glass bowl and microwave for 1 minute, until almost melted. Stir until the remaining bits melt and the chocolate is smooth, then set aside to cool slightly. Beat the cream cheese until smooth. Add the melted chocolate and beat again until smooth.

Add 1 cup of the icing sugar and stir until well blended. Add the remaining icing sugar and stir until you have a soft dough. Put a little extra icing sugar into a shallow dish. Shape the chocolate mixture into 1-inch balls and roll in the icing sugar to coat. Place on a sheet of waxed paper and refrigerate to firm them up a bit.

Makes 2 dozen truffles.

White Chocolate Peppermint Truffles

Roll the truffles in finely crushed candy canes or other peppermint candies instead of icing sugar. Fat content remains the same.

Dark Chocolate Cream Cheese Truffles

Use dark or semi-sweet chocolate chips or chunks in place of the white chocolate, and replace ¼ cup of the icing sugar with cocoa. Roll the truffles in cocoa instead. Fat content remains the same.

Ingredients

½ cup chopped white chocolate
4 oz light cream cheese, softened
2 cups icing sugar
extra icing sugar, for rolling

Nutrition Facts

Per truffle

Calories	68
Fat	2 g
Saturated	1.2 g
Monounsaturated	0.6 g
Polyunsaturated	0.1 g
Carbohydrates	12.3 g
Cholesterol	3.8 mg
Protein	0.7 g
Fiber	0 g
Calories from fat	26%

Fruitcake Drops

Gingerbread People

Chocolate Gingerbread

Mincemeat Cookies

Cranberry, Orange & White Chocolate Chunk Cookies

Fruitcake Brownies

Holiday Biscotti

Cranberry Pistachio Biscotti

Double Ginger Chews

Pear Mince Streusel Squares

Fruity Fig Newtons

Chocolate Mint Meringues

Eggnog Sugar Cookies

After Eight Sandwich Cookies

Chocolate Amaretti

Creamy Pumpkin Pie Squares

Chocolate Hazelnut Squares

Fresh Cranberry Orange Squares

Brandied Fruit Squares

Christmas Treats

Ingredients

1 cup mixed, diced candied
  citron
1 cup dark raisins
1 cup golden raisins
½ cup chopped, dried or candied cherries or cranberries
⅓ cup chopped walnuts or
  pecans
grated zest of an orange or
  lemon (optional)
½ cup orange juice or brandy
¼ cup water or orange juice
⅔ cup flour
½ tsp cinnamon
¼ tsp ground ginger
¼ tsp allspice
¼ tsp baking powder
¼ tsp salt
2 Tbsp butter or non-hydrogenated margarine, softened
¼ cup packed brown sugar
2 large egg whites
2 Tbsp corn syrup

Nutrition Facts

Per cookie

Calories	119
Fat	2.1 g
Saturated	0.7 g
Monounsaturated	0.5 g
Polyunsaturated	0.7 g
Carbohydrates	25 g
Cholesterol	2.6 mg
Protein	1.6 g
Fiber	1.4 g
Calories from fat	15%

Fruitcake Drops

No ambition to bake fruitcakes? It's much faster and easier with these bite-sized versions, which give the impression of fruitcake without the stigma of a dessert that could be used as a doorstop.

In a large bowl, combine the citron, raisins, golden raisins, cherries, nuts, zest, orange juice or brandy and water. Cover and let stand for several hours or overnight. Stir the mixture a few times as it sits.

In a small bowl, combine the flour, cinnamon, ginger, allspice, baking powder and salt; set aside.

In a large bowl, beat the butter and brown sugar until well blended. Beat in the egg whites and corn syrup until smooth.

Add the fruit mixture and flour mixture to the sugar mixture and stir just until combined. Cover and refrigerate for 1½–2 hours.

When you're ready to bake, preheat the oven to 350°F. Drop round spoonfuls of dough 1–2 inches apart on a cookie sheet sprayed with non-stick spray. Bake for 20–22 minutes, until the tops are just firm to the touch and no longer appear wet. Let cool on the sheet for a few minutes, then transfer to a wire rack to cool completely. If you like, sprinkle the cooled cookies with icing sugar.

Makes 2 dozen cookies.

Gingerbread People

During the holidays, everyone needs a recipe for gingerbread people. Of course the dough also makes great stars, trees and snowmen, and is worth the effort just for the way they make your house smell while they're baking. If you want to use fresh ginger, add about 2 tsp to the butter-sugar mixture.

In a large bowl, beat the butter, brown sugar, molasses and water with an electric mixer or by hand until smooth. In another large bowl, stir together the flour, baking soda, cinnamon, ginger, allspice, salt and cloves.

Add the flour mixture to the molasses mixture, stirring by hand just until you have a soft dough. Divide the dough in half, shape each piece into a disc, wrap in plastic and refrigerate for 2 hours or up to a few days.

When you're ready to bake, preheat the oven to 350°F.

On a lightly floured surface or between two pieces of waxed or parchment paper, roll one piece of dough out about ⅛ inch thick. Cut out with cookie cutters and place about an inch apart on a cookie sheet sprayed with non-stick spray.

Bake for 12–15 minutes, until set. Bake a few minutes longer for crispier cookies. Transfer to a wire rack to cool. Repeat with the remaining dough, re-rolling scraps once to get as many cookies as possible.

Makes 3 dozen cookies.

Ingredients

¼ cup butter, softened
½ cup packed brown sugar
¾ cup dark molasses
⅓ cup cold water
3½ cups all-purpose flour, or
   half all-purpose, half whole
   wheat
1 tsp baking soda
2 tsp cinnamon
1 tsp ground ginger
½ tsp allspice
½ tsp salt
¼ tsp ground cloves

Nutrition Facts
Per cookie

Calories	85
Fat	1.4 g
Saturated	0.8 g
Monounsaturated	0.4 g
Polyunsaturated	0.1 g
Carbohydrates	16.9 g
Cholesterol	3.5 mg
Protein	1.3 g
Fiber	0.4 g
Calories from fat	15%

Ingredients

1¼ cups flour
⅓ cup cocoa
½ tsp baking soda
¼ tsp baking powder
½ tsp cinnamon
½ tsp ground ginger
¼ tsp allspice
¼ tsp salt
pinch ground cloves
¼ cup butter or non-hydroge-
    nated margarine, softened
½ cup sugar
1 large egg white
¼ cup molasses
1 tsp vanilla

Nutrition Facts

Per cookie

Calories	46
Fat	1.4 g
Saturated	0.8 g
Monounsaturated	0.4 g
Polyunsaturated	0.1 g
Carbohydrates	8 g
Cholesterol	3.5 mg
Protein	0.7 g
Fiber	0.5 g
Calories from fat	26%

Chocolate Gingerbread

Chocolate and gingerbread go together so well I wonder why it isn't more common. The addition of chocolate makes gingerbread richer, deeper and more enticing than the usual cut-out gingerbread shapes, and cocoa doesn't add any fat.

In a medium bowl, combine the flour, cocoa, baking soda, baking powder, cinnamon, ginger, allspice, salt and cloves; set aside.

In a large bowl, beat the butter and sugar until creamy; add the egg white, molasses and vanilla and beat until smooth. Add the flour mixture and stir by hand just until you have a soft dough. Shape the dough into a disc, wrap in plastic and refrigerate for an hour or until well chilled.

When you're ready to bake, preheat the oven to 350°F. Roll out the dough between two sheets of waxed paper — or on a surface very lightly dusted with a combination of flour and sugar — until it's ⅛–¼-inch thick. Cut out the cookies using your choice of cookie cutters or a glass rim. Re-roll the scraps once to get as many cookies as possible.

Place the cookies an inch apart on a cookie sheet sprayed with non-stick spray. Bake for 10–12 minutes, until pale golden around the edges. Transfer to a wire rack to cool.

Makes 3 dozen cookies.

Chocolate Gingerbread Icebox Cookies

Shape the dough into a 12-inch log, wrap in waxed paper or plastic wrap and freeze for up to 3 months. Slice log into ¼-inch slices and bake as directed.

Mincemeat Cookies

Mince tarts are a must around my house at Christmas, but a little finicky to make, not to mention high-fat when using typical pastry. I made these one day when I was in a rush, and they were a hit.

In a large bowl, beat the butter, oil and sugar until well blended. The mixture will have the consistency of wet sand. Add the egg and vanilla and beat for a minute, until smooth and light.

Add the flour, baking powder and salt and stir by hand just until you have a soft dough. Wrap the dough in plastic wrap and refrigerate for about an hour, or overnight.

When you're ready to bake, preheat the oven to 350°F. Roll the chilled dough into 1½-inch balls, and place them about 2 inches apart on a cookie sheet sprayed with non-stick spray. Make an indent in the middle of each one with your thumb, and fill each hole with a small spoonful of mincemeat.

Bake for 12–15 minutes, until they've spread a bit and turned slightly golden around the edges. Transfer to a wire rack to cool.

Makes 1½ dozen cookies.

Ingredients

¼ cup butter, softened
1 Tbsp canola oil
¾ cup sugar
1 large egg
1 tsp vanilla
1½ cups all-purpose flour
½ tsp baking powder
¼ tsp salt
½ cup all-fruit mincemeat

Nutrition Facts
Per cookie

Calories	124
Fat	3.7 g
Saturated	1.7 g
Monounsaturated	1.3 g
Polyunsaturated	0.4 g
Carbohydrates	21 g
Cholesterol	19 mg
Protein	1.5 g
Fiber	0.5 g
Calories from fat	27%

Cranberry, Orange & White Chocolate Chunk Cookies

The creamy sweetness of white chocolate offset by the tartness of orange and cranberry makes these one of my favorite cookies, any time of year. Everyone who tries them goes crazy for them, too.

Preheat the oven to 350°F.

In a large bowl, beat the butter, sugar, brown sugar and orange zest until well blended. The mixture will look like wet sand. Add the egg, orange juice and vanilla and beat until smooth.

In a small bowl, stir together the flour, baking powder, baking soda and salt. Add to the sugar mixture and stir by hand until almost combined; add the cranberries and white chocolate and stir just until blended.

Drop spoonfuls of dough about 1 inch apart on a cookie sheet sprayed with non-stick spray. Bake for 12–14 minutes, until barely golden and set around the edges but still soft in the middle. Transfer to a wire rack to cool.

Makes 1½ dozen cookies.

Ingredients

¼ cup butter or non-hydrogenated margarine, softened
½ cup sugar
½ cup packed brown sugar
grated zest of 1 orange
1 large egg
3 Tbsp orange juice or thawed
   orange juice concentrate
1 tsp vanilla
1½ cups all-purpose flour
½ tsp baking powder
½ tsp baking soda
¼ tsp salt
1 cup fresh or frozen (unthawed) cranberries, left
   whole or coarsely chopped
½ cup white chocolate chunks
   or chips

Nutrition Facts

Per cookie

Calories	138
Fat	4.4 g
Saturated	2.5 g
Monounsaturated	1.3 g
Polyunsaturated	0.2 g
Carbohydrates	23.4 g
Cholesterol	20 mg
Protein	1.7 g
Fiber	0.6 g
Calories from fat	28%

Fruitcake Brownies

When I first heard about the potential marriage of fruitcake and brownies, I admit I wasn't tempted; I love both, but felt that one shouldn't interfere with the other. It turns out they're great together: both equally rich, dense and moist. Combining the two takes care of your chocolate fix while saving the time and expense of baking large batches of fruitcake.

In a large bowl or container, combine the cranberries, raisins and rum, and let soak for at least a couple of hours, or overnight. When you're ready to bake, drain them well and preheat the oven to 350°F.

In a large bowl, mix together the butter and sugar, then add the egg, egg whites, vanilla and coffee and stir until thoroughly blended and smooth.

In a medium bowl, stir together the flour, cocoa, baking powder and salt. Add to the egg mixture and stir by hand just until almost blended; add the soaked fruit and nuts and stir gently just until combined.

Spread the batter in an 8- × 8-inch pan sprayed with non-stick spray. Bake for 30–35 minutes, until the edges just begin to pull away from the sides of the pan, but the center is still slightly soft. Don't overbake. Cool in the pan on a wire rack.

Makes 16 brownies.

Ingredients

1 cup fresh or frozen cranberries, coarsely chopped
½ cup golden raisins
⅓ cup rum, brandy or orange juice
⅓ cup chopped walnuts or pecans
¼ cup butter or non-hydrogenated margarine, melted
1¼ cups sugar
1 large egg
2 large egg whites
1 tsp vanilla
1 tsp instant coffee granules, dissolved in 1 tsp water
1 cup all-purpose flour
½ cup cocoa
¼ tsp baking powder
¼ tsp salt

Nutrition Facts
Per brownie

Calories	170
Fat	5 g
Saturated	2.1 g
Monounsaturated	1.4 g
Polyunsaturated	1.2 g
Carbohydrates	28.6 g
Cholesterol	21.2 mg
Protein	3 g
Fiber	2.3 g
Calories from fat	26%

Ingredients

2 Tbsp butter or non-hydrogenated margarine, softened
¾ cup sugar
grated zest and juice of
    1 orange
2 large eggs
1 tsp vanilla
2 cups all-purpose flour
2 tsp baking powder
½ tsp cinnamon
¼ tsp allspice
¼ tsp salt
⅓ cup dried cranberries
⅓ cup white or semi-sweet
    chocolate chips
⅓ cup chopped walnuts
    or pecans

Nutrition Facts

Per biscotto

Calories	104
Fat	3.2 g
Saturated	1.2 g
Monounsaturated	0.9 g
Polyunsaturated	0.8 g
Carbohydrates	16.8 g
Cholesterol	21 mg
Protein	2.2 g
Fiber	0.6 g
Calories from fat	28%

Holiday Biscotti

If you're looking for shippable cookies during the holidays, these are sturdy and keep well, making them ideal for mailing. They're also great dunked in a mug of hot chocolate, warm tea or apple cider.

Preheat the oven to 350°F.

In a large bowl, beat the butter, sugar, eggs and vanilla until smooth. Add the flour, baking powder and salt and stir until almost combined; add the dried cranberries, chocolate chips and walnuts and stir just until blended. If it seems dry, use your hands to complete the mixing as the dough comes together.

Turn the dough out onto a floured surface. Divide in half and shape each piece into an 8-inch log. Place the logs 2–3 inches apart on a cookie sheet sprayed with non-stick spray, and flatten each into a rectangle that's about 3 inches wide.

Bake for 20–25 minutes, until firm and starting to crack on top. Transfer the logs to a wire rack to cool for a bit and reduce the oven temperature to 275°F.

When they're cool enough to handle (they tend to crumble when they're still hot), place the logs on a cutting board, trim the ends and cut each log diagonally into ½–¾-inch slices with a serrated knife.

Place the slices upright on the cookie sheet, spacing them about ½ inch apart so that there's room for the air to circulate between them, and return to the oven for 30 minutes. If you like, turn the heat off and leave the biscotti inside the oven until it cools down to make them even harder.

Makes 2 dozen biscotti.

Cranberry Pistachio Biscotti

You may substitute almonds, pecans or hazelnuts for the pistachios (all are very high in essential minerals such as magnesium, calcium and potassium), but the red and green bits make these ideal for the holidays. They're also fantastic with chunks of white chocolate.

Preheat the oven to 350°F.

In a large bowl, combine the oil, sugar, eggs and vanilla and stir until well blended.

In a medium bowl, stir together the flour, baking powder and salt. Add to the egg mixture along with the cranberries and pistachios and stir just until combined.

With slightly dampened hands, shape the dough into a 12-inch log and flatten it slightly so that it's about 4 inches wide. Place the log on a cookie sheet sprayed with non-stick spray and bake for 25–30 minutes, or until golden and firm.

Remove from the oven and set the log aside to cool for 20 minutes or so. Reduce the oven temperature to 275°F.

When the log is cool enough to handle (they tend to crumble when they're hot), transfer to a cutting board and cut it diagonally into ½–¾-inch slices with a serrated knife. Place the slices upright on the cookie sheet, spacing them about ½ inch apart so that there's room for the air to circulate between them, and return to the oven for 30 minutes. If you like, turn the heat off and leave the biscotti inside the oven until it cools down to make them even harder.

Makes 15 biscotti.

Ingredients

3 Tbsp canola oil
¾ cup sugar
2 large eggs
2 tsp vanilla
1¾ cups all-purpose flour
1 tsp baking powder
¼ tsp salt
½ cup dried cranberries
½ cup shelled pistachios, coarsely chopped

Nutrition Facts
Per biscotto

Calories	157
Fat	5.8 g
Saturated	0.7 g
Monounsaturated	3.4 g
Polyunsaturated	1.3 g
Carbohydrates	23.4 g
Cholesterol	28.7 mg
Protein	3 g
Fiber	1 g
Calories from fat	33%

Double Ginger Chews

Pillowy comfort cookies for ginger lovers; the cocoa adds depth and richness to them, not chocolate flavor. If you're really in it for the ginger, double the crystallized ginger and don't bother with the raisins.

Preheat the oven to 350°F.

In a large bowl, beat the butter and sugar until creamy. Add the molasses and egg and beat until smooth.

In a medium bowl, combine the flour, cocoa, cinnamon, ground ginger, baking soda and salt. Add the flour mixture to the molasses mixture and stir by hand until the dough starts to come together. Add the raisins, nuts and crystallized ginger (if using) and stir just until combined.

Drop large spoonfuls of dough about 2 inches apart on a cookie sheet sprayed with non-stick spray. Bake 12–14 minutes, until set around the edges but still slightly soft in the middle. Transfer to a wire rack to cool.

Makes 2 dozen cookies.

Ingredients

¼ cup butter or non-hydrogenated margarine, softened
½ cup sugar
¾ cup dark molasses
1 large egg
2 cups all-purpose flour
1 Tbsp cocoa
1 tsp cinnamon
1 tsp ground ginger
½ tsp baking soda
½ tsp salt
¼ cup finely chopped crystallized ginger
½ cup raisins or other dried
  fruit (optional)
⅓ cup chopped walnuts or
  pecans, toasted (optional)

Nutrition Facts

Per cookie

Calories	109
Fat	2.3 g
Saturated	1.3 g
Monounsaturated	0.7 g
Polyunsaturated	0.1 g
Carbohydrates	21.3 g
Cholesterol	14.2 mg
Protein	1.4 g
Fiber	0.5 g
Calories from fat	19%

Pear Mince Streusel Squares

Rather than open up a jar of mincemeat, chop up a few pears (they're extremely high in fiber, even more so if you leave them unpeeled), toss with some raisins, dried cranberries or any other dried fruit you like (figs are good), and use the mixture to make these squares in less time than it takes to do the pastry for mince tarts.

Preheat the oven to 350°F.

Peel, core and coarsely chop the pears. Coarsely chop the raisins and cranberries too. Toss them all together with the brown sugar, orange juice and cinnamon in a medium saucepan and bring to a boil over medium-high heat.

Reduce the heat and simmer, stirring occasionally, for 5 minutes or until the pears are tender. Remove from the heat.

In a large bowl, combine the flour, sugar and salt. Add the butter and orange juice and stir until the mixture is well combined and crumbly. Use your fingers to make sure the moisture is evenly distributed. It will resemble fresh bread crumbs.

Remove 1 cup of the crumbs and set them aside. Press the remaining crumbs into the bottom of an 8- × 8-inch pan sprayed with non-stick spray. Bake for 10–12 minutes, until pale golden around the edges.

Spread the pear mixture over the base and sprinkle with the remaining crumbs, squeezing the crumb mixture a little as you go. Bake for 30–35 minutes, until golden and bubbly around the edges. Cool in the pan on a wire rack.

Makes 16 squares.

Ingredients

Base & Topping
1½ cups flour
½ cup sugar
pinch salt
¼ cup butter, softened
1 Tbsp orange juice or milk

Filling
3 medium pears
⅓ cup raisins
⅓ cup dried cranberries
¼ cup packed brown sugar
2 Tbsp orange juice or brandy
½ tsp cinnamon

Nutrition Facts

Per square

Calories	137
Fat	3.1 g
Saturated	1.8 g
Monounsaturated	0.9 g
Polyunsaturated	0.2 g
Carbohydrates	26.7 g
Cholesterol	7.8 mg
Protein	1.5 g
Fiber	1.7 g
Calories from fat	20%

Ingredients

Pastry

1½ cups all-purpose flour
1 cup whole wheat flour
½ cup sugar
2 tsp baking powder
¼ tsp salt
¼ cup butter, chilled
¼ cup milk
1 large egg
1 large egg white
1 Tbsp canola oil
1 tsp vanilla

Filling

3 cups chopped dried figs
1½ cups raisins (or use half
    raisins and half dates)
1½ cups dried apricots
grated zest of 1 orange
½ cup chopped walnuts, ha-
    zelnuts or pecans, toasted
½ cup sugar
½ tsp cinnamon
½ cup orange juice or Marsala

Nutrition Facts

Per cookie

Calories	108
Fat	2.5 g
Saturated	0.3 g
Monounsaturated	1.2 g
Polyunsaturated	0.8 g
Carbohydrates	20.7 g
Cholesterol	5.2 mg
Protein	49.9 g
Fiber	1.5 g
Calories from fat	20%

Fruity Fig Newtons

Don't let the length of the ingredient list and instructions scare you, these are actually quite simple to make. Besides, baking elaborate cookies is much more fun during the holidays, and these put the packaged variety to shame.

To make the pastry, combine the flour, sugar, baking powder and salt in a food processor; pulse to mix. Add the butter and pulse to incorporate it. In a small bowl, whisk together the milk, egg, egg white, oil and vanilla. Pour the mixture through the feed tube with the processor running, mixing just until the dough comes together.

Shape the dough into a disc, wrap in plastic wrap and refrigerate overnight, or for up to 4 days.

To make the filling, place the figs, raisins, apricots, orange zest, nuts, sugar and cinnamon in the food processor (no need to wash it out) and pulse until the fruits and nuts are finely chopped. Pour orange juice or Marsala through the feed tube and process just until blended. Use immediately or cover and refrigerate for up to 3 days.

When you're ready to bake, preheat the oven to 375°F. Cut the dough into 6 equal pieces. On a lightly floured surface, roll each piece into a 4- × 12-inch rectangle, and spread about ¾ cup of the filling down the middle of each rectangle. Lift the sides of the dough over the filling to make a long roll, and pinch the edges to seal. Roll the log over and reshape to make it round.

Using a sharp serrated knife, trim the ends diagonally, then slice the cookies diagonally into 1-inch slices. Place them an inch apart on a cookie sheet that has been sprayed with non-stick spray.

Bake for 15–18 minutes, until golden. Transfer to a wire rack to cool. If you like, drizzle the cooled cookies with Vanilla Drizzle (page 200).

Makes 3½ dozen cookies.

Chocolate Mint Meringues

There aren't many things that are both fat-free and melt in your mouth, but egg whites and sugar combined—the basis for all meringues—does just that. Meringues are baked for a long time at a low temperature to make them crisp, and then cooled in the oven to dry them out. They shouldn't be sticky. If you want to bake the whole batch at once, spread the meringue in a thin layer over a prepared cookie sheet and bake as directed, then break into pieces like bark.

Preheat the oven to 225°F.

Line 2 baking sheets with parchment paper. Place the candy canes in a zip-lock bag and bash with a rolling pin until they're coarsely crushed.

Place the egg whites and cream of tartar in a clean glass or stainless steel bowl and beat at medium speed until soft peaks form. Increase the speed to high and gradually add the sugars, beating until stiff peaks form. Fold in the crushed candy and chocolate.

Drop the meringue mixture in spoonfuls onto the prepared sheets, swirling the tops. Bake for 1½ hours; turn the oven off and let them cool in the closed oven for 2 hours. Carefully peel the meringues from the paper.

Makes about 3 dozen meringues.

Chocolate Apricot Pecan Meringues
Replace the candy canes with ½ cup each coarsely chopped dried apricots and toasted pecans. Hazelnuts are good too! Bake as directed. Adds 1 g fat per meringue.

Coconut Meringues
Fold ½ tsp coconut extract and 1 cup toasted shredded coconut into the egg whites instead of the candy canes and chocolate. Bake as directed. Adds 0.7 g fat per meringue.

Ingredients

4 large egg whites
¼ tsp cream of tartar
½ cup sugar
¾ cup icing sugar
3 peppermint candy canes or hard peppermint candies
½ cup chocolate chips, coarsely chopped

Nutrition Facts
Per meringue

Calories	39
Fat	0.7 g
Saturated	0.4 g
Monounsaturated	0.2 g
Polyunsaturated	0 g
Protein	0.5 g
Carbohydrates	8.3 g
Cholesterol	0 mg
Fiber	0.1 g
Calories from fat	15%

Ingredients

¼ cup butter, softened
1 Tbsp canola oil
¾ cup sugar
1 large egg
1 tsp vanilla
1 tsp rum extract
1⅔ cups all-purpose flour
1 tsp baking powder
1 tsp cinnamon
½ tsp nutmeg
¼ tsp salt

Nutrition Facts

Per cookie

Calories	82
Fat	2.8 g
Saturated	1.3 g
Monounsaturated	1 g
Polyunsaturated	0.3 g
Carbohydrates	13 g
Cholesterol	14 mg
Protein	1.2 g
Fiber	0.3 g
Calories from fat	31%

Eggnog Sugar Cookies

Here's a fantastic alternative to the usual rolled sugar cookies or gingerbread; eggnog in crisp, buttery cookie form.

In a large bowl, beat the butter, oil and sugar with an electric mixer until well combined. Add the egg, vanilla and rum extract and beat for a minute, until smooth and light.

In a small bowl, stir together the flour, baking powder, cinnamon, nutmeg and salt. Add to the sugar mixture and stir by hand just until you have a soft dough. Shape the dough into a disc, wrap in plastic and refrigerate for an hour or until well chilled.

When you're ready to bake, preheat the oven to 350°F. Roll out the dough between two sheets of waxed paper—or on a surface very lightly dusted with a combination of flour and sugar—until it's ⅛–¼-inch thick. Cut out the cookies using a 2–3-inch cookie cutter or glass rim. Re-roll the scraps once to get as many cookies as possible.

Place the cookies an inch apart on a cookie sheet sprayed with non-stick spray. Bake for 10–12 minutes, until pale golden around the edges. Transfer to a wire rack to cool.

Makes 2 dozen cookies.

After Eight Sandwich Cookies

These crunchy chocolate sandwiches are made by squishing an After Eight chocolate-covered mint between two square chocolate cookies while they're still warm from the oven, melding them together in the most delicious way. It's the simplest way to make filled cookies.

In a large bowl, beat the butter, oil and sugar with an electric mixer until well combined. Add the egg and vanilla and beat for a minute, until smooth and light.

In a small bowl, stir together the flour, cocoa, baking powder and salt. Add to the sugar mixture and stir by hand just until you have a soft dough. Shape the dough into a disc, wrap in plastic and refrigerate for an hour or until well chilled.

When you're ready to bake, preheat the oven to 350°F. Roll out the dough between two sheets of waxed paper — or on a surface very lightly dusted with a combination of flour and sugar — until it's ⅛–¼-inch thick. Using a knife, cut the cookies into squares roughly the same size as the After Eight mints. Re-roll the scraps once to get as many cookies as possible.

Place the cookies an inch apart on a cookie sheet sprayed with non-stick spray. Bake for 10–12 minutes, until set. As soon as the cookies come out of the oven, place an After Eight mint between two cookies while they're still quite warm, squeeze a little to help the chocolate to melt, and set on a wire rack to cool.

Makes 20 sandwich cookies.

Ingredients

¼ cup butter, softened
1 Tbsp canola oil
¾ cup sugar
1 large egg
1 tsp vanilla or peppermint extract
1¼ cups all-purpose flour
½ cup cocoa
1 tsp baking powder
¼ tsp salt
15 After Eight mints

Nutrition Facts
Per cookie

Calories	107
Fat	4 g
Saturated	2 g
Monounsaturated	1.4 g
Polyunsaturated	0.4 g
Carbohydrates	18 g
Cholesterol	17 mg
Protein	1.7 g
Fiber	1.2 g
Calories from fat	32%

Chocolate Amaretti

These traditional Italian almond cookies resemble rich, chewy macaroons. Because 100% of the fat comes from the nuts, they're very low in saturated fat. They make a beautiful gift, packed in a box or tin lined with colored tissue paper.

Preheat the oven to 350°F.

Spread the almonds in a single layer on a cookie sheet and toast for 7–10 minutes, or until pale golden and fragrant. Remove from the sheet to cool completely, and reduce the oven temperature to 325°F. Line a cookie sheet with foil, and spray the foil with non-stick spray.

Put the almonds and 2 Tbsp of the sugar into a food processor. Pulse until the nuts are finely ground, being careful not to turn them into a paste. Add cocoa and icing sugar, and pulse to blend well.

In a medium glass or stainless steel bowl, beat the egg whites until foamy. Add the cream of tartar and beat until soft peaks form. Gradually add the remaining sugar, beating until stiff peaks form. Gently fold in the nut mixture, vanilla and almond extract.

Spoon the mixture into a large pastry bag fitted with a ½-inch tip, and pipe 1½-inch mounds on the cookie sheet, spacing them 1 inch apart. Alternatively, shape mounds with a spoon and your fingers.

Bake for 10–12 minutes, until crispy and firm to the touch. Transfer the entire sheet of foil to a wire rack to cool. Once they've cooled, gently peel the amaretti from the foil. Store extras in an airtight container.

Makes 1½ dozen amaretti.

Ingredients

1 cup blanched almonds
  (whole or slivered)
½ cup sugar
2 Tbsp cocoa
2 Tbsp icing sugar
2 large egg whites
⅛ tsp cream of tartar
½ tsp vanilla
½ tsp almond extract (optional)

Nutrition Facts

Per amaretti

Calories	75
Fat	4.3 g
Saturated	0.4 g
Monounsaturated	2.8 g
Polyunsaturated	0.9 g
Carbohydrates	8.3 g
Cholesterol	0 mg
Protein	2.2 g
Fiber	1.2 g
Calories from fat	48%

Creamy Pumpkin Pie Squares

Studies have shown that male arousal is triggered most by the aroma of pumpkin pie—more so than by the smell of flowers, musk, or any other scent we pay big bucks for. Turns out, all you need to do is bake something pumpkin-and-spicey. These fit the bill when you don't really want to make pie, or want something more portable.

Preheat the oven to 350°F.

In a medium bowl, stir together the butter and brown sugar until creamy. Add the flour and salt and stir until well combined and crumbly.

Press into the bottom of an 8- × 8-inch pan sprayed with non-stick spray. Bake for 8–10 minutes, until just barely golden around the edges.

In a medium bowl, stir together the condensed milk, pumpkin, brown sugar, egg, cinnamon, nutmeg, cloves and salt until smooth. Pour over the base.

Bake for an hour, until slightly puffed and set. Cool in the pan on a wire rack. Store extras covered in the refrigerator.

Makes 12 squares.

Ingredients

Base
¼ cup butter, softened
¼ cup packed brown sugar
1 cup flour
pinch salt

Filling
1 can sweetened condensed milk
one 14-oz (398-mL) can pumpkin
2 Tbsp packed brown sugar
1 large egg
½ tsp cinnamon
¼ tsp nutmeg
pinch ground cloves
pinch salt

Nutrition Facts
Per cookie

Calories	148
Fat	5 g
Saturated	3 g
Monounsaturated	1.4 g
Polyunsaturated	0.3 g
Carbohydrates	23.5 g
Cholesterol	27.7 mg
Protein	3 g
Fiber	0.7 g
Calories from fat	30%

Ingredients

Base

¼ cup butter, softened
¼ cup sugar
1 cup flour
pinch salt

Topping

1½ cups packed brown sugar
¼ cup cocoa
1 Tbsp flour
¼ tsp baking powder
¼ tsp salt
2 large eggs
1 tsp vanilla
1 cup hazelnuts, toasted,
    skinned and coarsely
    chopped

Nutrition Facts

Per square

Calories	208
Fat	8.6 g
Saturated	1 g
Monounsaturated	6.2 g
Polyunsaturated	0.9 g
Carbohydrates	31.8 g
Cholesterol	13.5 mg
Protein	98.1 g
Fiber	1.4 g
Calories from fat	36%

Chocolate Hazelnut Squares

If you replace the pecans with hazelnuts and add cocoa to the brown sugar filling, you end up with these chocolate-hazelnut squares that are low in saturated fat but an excellent source of heart-healthy monounsaturated fat. People who eat nuts on a regular basis significantly reduce their risk of heart disease and heart attacks.

Preheat the oven to 350°F.

In a medium bowl, stir together the butter and brown sugar until creamy. Add the flour and salt and stir until well combined and crumbly.

Press into the bottom of an 8- × 8-inch pan sprayed with non-stick spray. Bake for 8–10 minutes, until just barely golden around the edges.

In the same bowl (no need to wash it), combine the brown sugar, cocoa, flour, baking powder and salt. Add the eggs and vanilla and stir until well blended and smooth. Stir in the hazelnuts. Pour over the base and smooth the top. Bake for 30–35 minutes, until the top is slightly puffed and cracked, and looks dry. Cool completely in the pan on a wire rack.

Makes 16 squares.

CLOCKWISE FROM TOP: Chocolate Hazelnut
Squares p. 192; Pecan Pie Squares p. 132;
Hello Dollies p. 128

Fresh Cranberry Orange Squares

Ingredients

Base
¼ cup butter, softened
¼ cup sugar
1 cup flour
pinch salt

Filling
1½ cups fresh or frozen
    cranberries
grated zest and juice of 1
    orange
¼ cup sugar
1 cup packed brown sugar
2 Tbsp flour
½ tsp baking powder
¼ tsp salt
1 large egg
1 tsp vanilla

Nutrition Facts
Per square

Calories	145
Fat	3.3 g
Saturated	1.9 g
Monounsaturated	1 g
Polyunsaturated	0.2 g
Carbohydrates	28 g
Cholesterol	21.2 mg
Protein	1.4 g
Fiber	0.7 g
Calories from fat	20%

These chewy brown sugar-topped squares are reminiscent of butter tarts, but with a topping infused with orange and loaded with fresh cranberries. Add some chopped pecans too, if you like.

Preheat the oven to 350°F.

In a medium bowl, stir together the butter and sugar until creamy. Add the flour and salt and stir until well combined and crumbly.

Press into the bottom of an 8- × 8-inch pan sprayed with non-stick spray. Bake for 8–10 minutes, until just barely golden around the edges.

In a medium saucepan, cook the cranberries, orange zest, juice and sugar over medium-low heat until the skins pop, stirring often. This should take about 10 minutes. Remove from the heat and set aside to cool.

In the same bowl (no need to wash it), stir together the brown sugar, flour, baking powder and salt. Add the eggs and vanilla and stir in the cooled cranberry mixture. Spread over the crust.

Return to the oven for 30–35 minutes, until golden and bubbly around the edges. Cool completely in the pan on a wire rack.

Makes 16 squares.

Brandied Fruit Squares

People make a big deal about eating too much of whatever isn't good for them during the holidays, but dried fruits and nuts are as seasonal as chocolate and eggnog, and are some of the best foods to include in our diets. I love making recipes that include a colorful jumble of both; in these squares chewy-sweet fruit and crunchy nuts are balanced on a shortbread base that contains half the fat of most shortbread crusts.

Preheat the oven to 350°F.

In a medium saucepan, combine the golden and dark raisins, cranberries, apricots and brandy and bring to a boil. Immediately remove from the heat and set aside for 20 minutes; by then almost all of the liquid should be absorbed.

In a medium bowl, stir together the butter and brown sugar until creamy. Add the flour and salt and stir until well combined and crumbly. Press into the bottom of an 8- × 8-inch pan sprayed with non-stick spray. Bake for 8–10 minutes, until just barely golden around the edges.

In a medium bowl, beat the egg and egg white with an electric mixer for 2–3 minutes, until thick and foamy. In a small bowl combine the brown sugar, flour and salt. Add the sugar mixture and vanilla to the eggs and stir just until combined. Stir in the fruit mixture. Spread evenly over the crust and sprinkle with walnuts.

Bake for 30–35 minutes, until golden and set. If you need to, cover with foil for the last 10 minutes to prevent them from browning too much. Cool in the pan on a wire rack. Sprinkle with icing sugar before or after cutting into squares.

Makes 16 squares.

Ingredients

Base
¼ cup butter, softened
⅓ cup packed brown sugar
1 cup flour
pinch salt

Topping
½ cup packed golden raisins
½ cup packed dark raisins
½ cup packed dried cranberries
½ cup packed chopped dried apricots
½ cup brandy or orange juice
1 large egg
1 large egg white
1 cup packed brown sugar
¼ cup flour
¼ tsp salt
1 tsp vanilla
⅓ cup chopped walnuts or pecans
icing sugar, for sprinkling

Nutrition Facts

Per square

Calories	198
Fat	4.8 g
Saturated	2 g
Monounsaturated	1.3 g
Polyunsaturated	1.2 g
Carbohydrates	37.7 g
Cholesterol	31.2 mg
Protein	2.8 g
Fiber	2 g
Calories from fat	21%

Fluffy White Marshmallow Frosting

Lemon Cream Cheese Frosting

Peanut Butter Frosting

Maple Frosting

Vanilla Drizzle

Smooth Decorating Icing

Brown Sugar Frosting

Icings, Frostings
& Drizzles

Ingredients

2 large egg whites
1½ cups sugar
¼ tsp cream of tartar (optional)
1 Tbsp light corn syrup
⅓ cup water

Nutrition Facts

Per tablespoon

Calories	26
Fat	0 g
Carbohydrates	6.6 g
Cholesterol	0 mg
Protein	0 g
Fiber	0 g

Fluffy White Marshmallow Frosting

This is my absolute favorite frosting. It's pure white, smooth and creamy, with a marshmallowy texture, and unlike most frostings, fat free! If you want color, just add a drop or two of food coloring to the water.

In a large stainless steel or glass bowl, or in the bowl of a double boiler, combine the egg whites, sugar, cream of tartar, corn syrup and water. Place the bowl over a pot with about an inch of boiling water in it, and beat on high speed with an electric mixer for 7–8 minutes, until stiff peaks form. Remove the bowl from the heat immediately.

Makes 3 cups.

Ingredients

¼ cup light cream cheese, softened
2 Tbsp butter or non-hydrogenated margarine, softened
1 Tbsp lemon juice
1½ cups icing sugar

Nutrition Facts

Per tablespoon

Calories	43
Fat	1.4 g
Saturated	0.9 g
Monounsaturated	0.4 g
Polyunsaturated	0.1 g
Carbohydrates	7.6 g
Cholesterol	4 mg
Protein	0.2 g
Fiber	0 g
Calories from fat	29%

Lemon Cream Cheese Frosting

Cream cheese frosting goes well with more than just carrot cake; try it with any spiced cookie, or replace the lemon juice with water and spread it on chocolate cookies or brownies.

In a medium bowl, beat the cream cheese and butter until smooth and fluffy. Add the lemon juice and icing sugar and beat until smooth, adding a little extra lemon juice or water and icing sugar if you need it to make a spreadable frosting.

Makes about 1½ cups, enough to frost a pan of squares or about 2 dozen cookies.

Peanut Butter Frosting

Peanut Butter Frosting goes perfectly with flavors from banana to chocolate to caramel. Use regular or all-natural peanut butter if that's what you have.

Beat the peanut butter and butter until smooth; add the icing sugar and milk and beat until you have a smooth, spreadable frosting. Add a little extra icing sugar or milk as needed to achieve the right consistency.

Makes about 1½ cups, enough to frost a pan of squares or about 2 dozen cookies.

Ingredients

¼ cup light peanut butter
1 Tbsp butter, softened
1¾ cups icing sugar
¼ cup milk
1 tsp vanilla

Nutrition Facts
Per tablespoon

Calories	52
Fat	1.4 g
Saturated	0.5 g
Monounsaturated	0.5 g
Polyunsaturated	0.3 g
Carbohydrates	9.7 g
Cholesterol	1.4 mg
Protein	0.6 g
Fiber	0 g
Calories from fat	23%

Maple Frosting

Regular maple-flavored table syrup works fine, but pure maple syrup has a far better flavor.

In a bowl, beat the butter, milk, vanilla and icing sugar until well combined. Gradually add the syrup, beating as you pour it in, until your frosting is smooth and spreadable.

Makes about 2 cups, enough to frost 2 pans of squares or about 3 dozen cookies.

Ingredients

2 Tbsp butter, softened
3–4 Tbsp milk
½ tsp vanilla or maple extract
2 cups icing sugar
⅓–½ cup pure maple syrup

Nutrition Facts
Per tablespoon

Calories	52
Fat	1.4 g
Saturated	0.5 g
Monounsaturated	0.5 g
Polyunsaturated	0.3 g
Carbohydrates	13 g
Cholesterol	2.7 mg
Protein	0.1 g
Fiber	0 g
Calories from fat	15%

Ingredients

1 cup icing sugar
½ tsp vanilla
2 Tbsp milk

Nutrition Facts

Per tablespoon

Calories	30
Fat	0 g
Carbohydrates	7.6 g
Cholesterol	0 mg
Protein	0 g
Fiber	0 g

Vanilla Drizzle

Try using other extracts—such as almond, maple, rum or coconut—instead of the vanilla for a different flavor.

Combine all the ingredients in a medium bowl and mix until smooth, adding a little extra liquid or sugar if needed to achieve a drizzling consistency.

Chocolate Drizzle

Add 2–3 Tbsp cocoa to the mixture. Fat content remains the same.

Maple Drizzle

Add 2 Tbsp maple syrup, and reduce the milk by about half. Fat content remains the same.

Orange or Lemon Drizzle

Replace the milk with lemon juice or thawed orange juice concentrate. Fat content remains the same.

Coffee Drizzle

Add 1 Tbsp instant coffee to the milk. Fat content remains the same.

Smooth Decorating Icing

Because it dries completely and isn't sticky, this is the perfect icing for cookies meant to be decorations or ornaments. Because she made it popular, I call it Martha Stewart icing.

Combine all the ingredients, using just a drop or two of food coloring if you want some color, and stir until completely smooth. Add a drop or two of water or a small amount of icing sugar if necessary to achieve a slightly fluid, spreadable consistency.

Lightly spread the icing on completely cooled cookies. If you're using sprinkles or other decorations, put them on right away before the icing sets.

Makes about 2 cups, enough to frost about 2½ dozen cookies.

Ingredients

2½ cups icing sugar
¼ cup hot water
1 tsp light corn syrup
¼ tsp vanilla
food coloring (optional)

Nutrition Facts

Per serving, based on 2½ dozen cookies

Calories	40
Fat	0 g
Carbohydrates	10 g
Cholesterol	0 mg
Protein	0 g
Fiber	0 g

Brown Sugar Frosting

Brown sugar frosting, also known as penuche, has a caramel flavor that goes well with any kind of cookie

Combine the butter, brown sugar and milk in a small saucepan set over medium heat. Cook, stirring often, until the butter and sugar are completely melted, but don't let it boil for too long or you'll end up with candy!

Transfer the mixture to a bowl and add the icing sugar. Beat on low speed, adding a little extra milk if you need it, until the frosting is smooth and spreadable.

Makes about 1½ cups, enough to frost a pan of squares or about 2 dozen cookies.

Ingredients

1 Tbsp butter or non-hydrogenated margarine, softened
¼ cup packed brown sugar
3 Tbsp milk
1½ cups icing sugar

Nutrition Facts

Per tablespoon

Calories	43
Fat	0.5 g
Saturated	0.3 g
Monounsaturated	0.1 g
Polyunsaturated	0 g
Carbohydrates	9.8 g
Cholesterol	1.4 mg
Protein	0.1 g
Fiber	0 g
Calories from fat	10%

Conversion Charts

Imperial	Metric
¼ tsp	1 mL
½ tsp	2.5 mL
1 tsp	5 mL
1 Tbsp	15 mL
¼ cup	60 mL
⅓ cup	80 mL
½ cup	120 mL
⅔ cup	160 mL
¾ cup	180 mL
1 cup	240 mL

Imperial		Metric
oz	lb	gm
¼ oz	–	7 gm
½ oz	–	15 gm
1 oz	–	30 gm
2 oz	–	55 gm
4 oz	¼ lb	110 gm
5 oz	–	140 gm
8 oz	½ lb	230 gm
10 oz	–	280 gm
16 oz	1 lb	450 gm
24 oz	1½ lb	680 gm
32 oz	2 lb	900 gm

Fahrenheit	Celsius
175	80
200	95
225	110
250	120
275	140
300	150
325	160
350	180
375	190
400	200
425	220
450	230

Index